PRINCIPAL

MATTERS

THE MOTIVATION, COURAGE, AND ACTION NEEDED FOR SCHOOL LEADERSHIP

William D. Parker

DEDICATION

To my beautiful wife, Missy, whose friendship and love
these past twenty years have given me the freedom and
courage to follow and to lead. And to our children Emily,
Mattie, Katie, and Jack who have filled our lives with
unbelievable joy in the journey.

Praise For *Principal Matters*

―――――――――◦―――――――――

"This book captures the essence of effective teamwork and leadership. A great read for school administrators!"

- **Annette Breaux, educator, co-author with Todd Whitaker of *The Ten-Minute Inservice***

―――――――――――――――――――

"Will is a great storyteller, and his use of these connections makes this book easy to read but also memorable. His focus on 'purpose'—going beyond what you do in school—is something that all leaders should really consider if they are going to make a difference in both their professional and personal lives."

- **George Couros, Principal, founder of ConnectedPrincipals.com, and an Innovative Teaching, Learning and Leadership consultant**

―――――――――――――――――――

"Will generously shares experiences from his personal and professional life to remind principals of the big picture as well as the small details that are essential to the success of our school communities…Being a school leader can be lonely work, as the role of principal is only truly understood by those who have served in the position. Mr. Parker has utilized his time occupying the principal's office to develop practical yet inspiring tips for administrators. I'm excited to politely steal many of his great ideas with my own students and staff this school year!"

- **Rachel Skerritt, Principal of Eastern Senior High School, a D.C. Public School. 2013 Principal Ambassador Fellow for the U.S. Department of Education**

"Will writes with passion, conviction and insight. This book will equip you with the tools you'll need to face the frustrations you're sure to encounter as an educator, while enabling to you find renewed purpose and meaning as you influence your students to be the best they can be."

- **Daniel Wong, author of *The Happy Student***

"This book explains the <u>why</u> of school leadership, not just the <u>how</u>. If you want to understand the right motives for school leadership and the steps to being a successful principal, you should read, *Principal Matters* by William D. Parker."

– Jon Gordon, author of *The Energy Bus* and *Soup*

CONTENTS

Part I   The Foundation

Part 2   Action Steps

Part 5 A Place Of Belonging

ACKNOWLEDGMENTS

This book is the product of lots of questions from fellow educators and school leaders that I finally decided to answer. I am indebted to my friends, colleagues and leaders who invested in me in my growth and who continue to challenge and encourage me. I am also thankful for my wife and children and my extended family back home as well as my church family. And I am grateful for my students and school community for giving me the opportunity to serve. It is truly a pleasure to do something together that matters.

Preface:
Learning To Lead A School

I n 1975 Diana Nyad slipped into the cool waters off the Manhattan shore and began a 28-mile swim around the island that would become her first world record swim. In 1979 she set another record with a 102-mile trek from the Bahamas to Florida.

At age 60, after not swimming for decades, but staying active in other sports, she made it a personal goal to set a world record by swimming from Cuba to Florida.

Her 100-mile feat came after years of unsuccessful attempts, the pain of jelly-fish attacks, hallucinations, and unwavering teamwork.

At age 64, she achieved her dream.

When Diana Nyad was interviewed after making shore, she said two things. One, *never ever give up*. And, two, *teamwork*.[1]

As a school leader, you may not face attacking jellyfish, but you will encounter some tough challenges ahead. Whether it is an unexpected crisis, a difficult parent, or a rigorous program, you will face rough waters.

You will also experience some great successes.

Like long-distance swimming, being a school leader is a marathon, not a sprint.

And if you take nothing else away from glancing at this introduction, remember two things: To be a school leader, you must have courage, and you must believe in teamwork.

Why I Wrote This Book

---

[1] "Diana Nyad." *TED: Ideas worth Spreading.* Web. Dec. 2013. <https://www.ted.com/speakers/diana_nyad>.

Over the years, I have met a lot of school leaders. Many were great at their jobs, and some weren't. Many loved their jobs, and some didn't.

Although I don't pretend anyone can be great at every aspect of job, or love it every day, I do believe that strong leaders achieve meaningful results by understanding their goals, counting the costs, running the race with endurance, and surrounding themselves with gifted team members.

You see, Diane Nyad didn't finish her race by gliding solo through the water, a solitary figure in the vast ocean blue.

She was amazingly courageous and gifted, but also she was surrounded by boats of specialists in navigation, medicine, sea-life, nutrition, communication, etc.

If you are reading this book, it is likely you are a school leader or aspiring to be one. The lessons I share in the pages ahead are ones I have learned the hard way, through trial and error, success and failure. And they were learned from being surrounded by fellow school leaders, my school teammates, my students, and my school community.

But even with all the support, leadership can still be a lonely calling at times. That's why it also requires courage. Someone has to make the final decision, and often you are the one.

If you are willing to take the plunge into the waters of school leadership, read ahead. If so, I will give you practical tips on understanding your motivation, how to handle crisis, how to deal with difficult people, how to communicate effectively, how to identify your team's key responsibility areas, and so much more.

I am no Diana Nyad. My name is not listed in a hall of fame. But as I have met fellow school leaders over the years, I have heard some consistent themes in the challenges they face. This book is my attempt to offer some advice from my twenty plus years in education and school leadership.

How This Book Is Organized

This book is written so that each chapter can be read in one sitting. Although it is organized with specific subjects in mind, each chapter is a lesson in itself.

At the end of each chapter is a section entitled "Now It's Your Turn," where I ask questions to encourage you to take action on what you are learning.

About The Author

I have been an educator for twenty years, first as a high school English teacher, then as a high school assistant principal, and now as a high school principal.

I grew up as a farm boy from west Tennessee and never thought I would go to college. But I loved to learn and eventually found myself in Oklahoma with a degree in hand and classrooms full of students who taught me more about teaching (and life) than I ever expected.

In 1998, I was named Teacher of the Year at the high

school where I taught. In 2012, I had the honor of being named the Oklahoma Assistant Principal of the Year. I am currently the principal of Skiatook High School, near Tulsa, Oklahoma, U.S.A.

On the home front, my wife and I have been happily married for more than twenty years, and we are the proud parents of four children: three girls and one boy.

My goal is to inspire innovative ideas for school leaders. I also write because it motivates me to keep growing. I hope you find this book motivation for yourself, your leadership, and your school. You can find out more about my resources for school leaders at my website: www.williamdparker.com.

Introduction:
One Day As A Principal

———— ∼ ————

Sometimes people ask me what a "typical day" looks like for a principal. Instead of beginning with a list of a principal's responsibilities, perhaps an example of one day from my school year may serve as a better illustration. Every day is different for me, but here is one:

5:15 AM I am up and dressed for time on the treadmill while listening to an audio-Bible app. I breakfast, read, shower and get ready for the day.

6:30 AM On the road to school. Listening to morning news or podcast on the commute while my 9th grade daughter falls sleeps in the passenger seat beside me.

7:00 AM Opening up the office, turning on lights in

the commons area. Early-arriving student drops in to tell me about a book he is reading and just wants to hang out a while before eating breakfast.

7:15 AM While I chat with student, I sign substitute forms; teachers come to sign in. The cafeteria is starting to fill with other early-arrivals.

7:35 AM In cafeteria while more students arrive for breakfast. Talking to assistant principals about the day. Parent and student come in and wait for a meeting I will be attending in 10 minutes with the student's special education teacher and others.

7:45 AM Secretary tells me a parent is on the line wanting to talk about bullying incident on a bus. Number taken so one of the assistant principals or I can call back after IEP.

7:47 AM I'm late to the IEP meeting but catch up as we discuss the student's grade. His single dad is worried because his son is behind on credits and is not taking seriously his responsibility to hand in all assignments. We coach, cajole, and counsel.

8:30 AM Back in my office. Parent with bullying concern is now at the school and meeting with one of my assistant principals.

Fill in my secretary on which classrooms I plan to visit today. Answer questions about calendar requests for use of auditorium. Check voicemail and forward transcript request from out-of-state school to our registrar. Answer email question from business office concerning teacher certification.

9:00 AM I am in a classroom observing a teacher and logging areas on our state-mandated teacher observation instrument. I am trying to use my iPad but the log-in for the online observation instrument is not working, so I email them for help and finish my notes on paper so that I can follow up later.

10:00 AM I am in the hallways for the passing period. Then I am reminding the student making daily announcements to give a shout-out to the freshman boy basketball players who are in a tournament. I say hello to a therapist who comes to the school to meet with some students. I touch base with my assistant principals about the bullying report and other items they have dealt with this morning.

10:15 AM I return a phone call to parent of a student we emergency suspended and finalize an upcoming meeting date. School counselor stops me to ask some questions about course selections on our information-system not coded correctly. This prompts another conversation about a conflict in the flowchart for traditional and advanced coursework. We set up a meeting to discuss and find a solution.

11:00 AM I am in another classroom doing my observation in writing because the online version is still not working.

11:45 AM I am in the lunchroom for second lunch helping with supervision and watching as students put donations in boxes for a fund-raiser. The teacher who gets the most money in their box will get a pie in the face. I have a box there with my name on it. I eat lunch and think about pie.

12:30 PM I meet with our SRO (Student Resource Officer) who informs me about a situation that will require police presence to interview a student with the student parent present. We call the student out of class and facilitate the meeting.

1:30 PM I have called my superintendent to give him a heads-up on the situation because a parent has said she is contacting the media over the incident that happened on a school bus. I answer questions about student situation from a teacher who has stopped by on his planning period.

2:00 PM I read emails and call the state department to ask a question about a report detail. I respond to an invitation to an upcoming conference. I approve two maintenance requests, and a transportation request. I sign time sheets for our custodians and support staff, substitute forms, purchase order requests, and calendar requests.

I agree to a meeting with an insurance agent who wants to visit to discuss services he provides for schools. I meet with a senior student who needs a letter of recommendation.

2:50 PM School dismisses and I walk the commons and bus stop areas to supervise. I answer more email questions from teachers. I text my wife about evening plans. I eat a snack. I work on a PowerPoint for an upcoming workshop.

4:00 PM I go to the school gym and watch a girl's basketball scrimmage where my daughter participates. I talk with our athletic director and check a few more emails on my iPad.

5:30 PM My daughter and I stop for a quick bite on our way to a boy's basketball game. The junior high and freshman boys are in a tournament.

8:00 PM The freshman boys game started late because one of the junior high games went into over-time. While watching the game, I catch up with a staff member on some happenings in the office that will need my attention tomorrow.

9:30 PM I am home in time to kiss my 8-year old son good night and touch base with my two younger daughters who are already in bed.

10:30 PM Before sleeping, my wife and I talk about events of the day. I check my personal emails (which I keep on a separate account from my school email). I update a blog draft and plug in my cell phone before sleeping.

Wrap It Up

Not all days are like this for a principal. Some are crazier and some less hectic. Nevertheless, being a principal means constant change and problem solving.

What you have to guard against is losing sight of reaching specific short-term and long-term goals in the constant demand of addressing urgent or immediate requests.

So, how do school leaders keep perspective with so

many demands?

Before we start discussing practical suggestions, I want to take time to discuss ideas that are more foundational to school leadership. I want to talk about motivation, purpose, wonder, and perspective.

Now It's Your Turn

School leaders wear lots of different hats throughout the day. How do you plan and prioritize in the midst of so many demands? What priorities will keep you going even during difficult days?

Part I
The Foundation

Chapter 1
Purpose-Driven Leadership

———~———

I once heard a great interview of Lisa Earle McLeod discussing her book *Selling With Noble Purpose.*[2]

The premise of the conversation was that in corporations, the sales reps who make up the top 2% of highest achievers share a surprising similarity: without exception, each one was motivated more by purpose than profit.

And guess what? In the process, they profited more! The same is true in school.

A Quick Story

---

[2] McLeod, Lisa Earle. *Selling with Noble Purpose: How to Drive Revenue and Do Work That Makes You Proud.* Hoboken, NJ: John Wiley & Sons, 2013. Print.

We have a student who is an orphan at my school. She struggles with so many emotions and doesn't always make the best decisions—even though she is finally passing all her classes.

One day I met with her after she had skipped school, and I assigned her to our ISP room (one teacher/no social interaction for the day) for discipline.

When she caught up on her work, she asked if she could read something, so I sent her *Chicken Soup for the Teenage Soul*.[3] She asked to see me later in the day.

When she came into my office, she told me that she had read the entire book and wanted more. So our librarian sent over a copy of *Chicken Soup for the Woman's Soul*.[4] She asked if she could take it home. When I told her the librarian said

---

[3] Canfield, Jack, Mark Victor. Hansen, and Kimberly Kirberger. *Chicken Soup for the Teenage Soul: 101 Stories of Life, Love, and Learning*. Deerfield Beach, FL: Health Communications, 1997. Print.

[4] Canfield, Jack. *Chicken Soup for the Woman's Soul: 101 Stories to Open the Hearts and Rekindle the Spirits of Women*. Deerfield Beach, FL: Health Communications, 1996. Print.

she could have it for two weeks, she clutched it to her chest and beamed.

"Awesome!" she shouted.

You would have thought it was a Christmas present.

Sometimes you will have days when you don't enjoy what you do. Keeping track of all the demands—dealing with discipline decisions, for instance, can be wearing. But in moments like these, you must first remember why you are here.

Each of us can enjoy work more when we remember it has a purpose.

The same holds true for every occupation. Whether it's providing safer designs through engineering, better care through medicine, excellent service and entertainment through running a restaurant—whatever the vocation, God gifts us to make better the world around us.

But to be a strong leader, you have to keep your purpose firmly fixed in mind.

Ask Yourself This Question

What is the purpose that is driving you each day as a school leader? If you don't answer this question, you will find yourself overwhelmed by the journey ahead or simply counting the days until retirement.

As I have wrestled with the question of purpose, I have settled on two motivations that keep me going:

1. My job is to help create a place of security, stability, meaning, and mission.
2. My job is to redeem, repair, rescue, and rebuild what is broken or in need of improvement.

I could talk in detail about each of the above, but instead, let me challenge you to look around your school and ask yourself, "How is what I am doing today going to help create the best environment for learning and help those who are struggling?"

When you walk through your day remembering that your purpose is more than just raising test scores or "putting out fires"–when you discover the joy of supporting team members or helping students discover the wonder of learning, then you tap into your purpose.

And like my orphan student had found stories that gripped her heart, purpose is something that will keep you motivated in leadership

In all the do's and don'ts of school leadership, don't forget the higher purpose of being called *to serve*. A school leader's profit margins may not be the same as a corporate sales rep. But the benefits you receive from watching students succeed are something money can't buy. Let that be the first of lessons you take into your leadership journey.

Now It's Your Turn

Think back to an experience that has reminded you of your purpose in your position. What happened to remind you of your purpose? What are some ways you have learned to hold on to that focus?

Chapter 2
Caution Lights On Your Journey

———————⌁———————

I want to stay on the theme of purpose-driven leadership because it is so foundational to learning to lead with fulfillment.

Leadership coaches like Chris Locurto refer to Zig Ziglar's "wheel of life"[5] because it represents a good visual of the competing interests in each of our lives.

———————————

[5] Locurto, Chris. "Zig Ziglar's Wheel of Life." Chris Locurto. 11 May 2011. Web. <http://chrislocurto.com/zig-ziglars-wheel-of-life/>.

The thought goes, when the areas of life are held in good balance, the ride is much smoother. When one area of life is off-balance, we experience a flat tire.

Although it is safe to say that none of us has a perfectly balanced life, I almost made a fatal assumption in my early years of school leadership by thinking if I worked harder, I would accomplish more.

I believed managing the needs of students, teachers, staff, parents, etc. required every second of school as well as hours before and after.

As a result, I consistently worked through lunches or skipped dinners to keep up with the demands.

Eventually, this pace led to burnout. And a leader who burns out is a miserable leader…and eventually so are those around you.

Analyzing Your Own Work/Life Balance

Do you often feel driven to work harder and harder to reach your goals? You may be in danger of burning out before ever reaching the most important goals.

Here are some caution-lights want you to keep in mind

as you walk your leadership journey:

1. Recognize the Danger-Signs of Work-a-holism.

As I discovered the havoc over-work was creating in my life, my wife told me one day, "The kids and I have resigned ourselves to having a weekend husband and father. And even then, you are pretty much a shell of the man you were before."

This was a wake-up call for me to revisit my priorities. Did I want to grow older and find myself with a successful career only to find my wife and children no longer knew me?

As I worked harder and harder at my school, I was growing weaker in other areas of my life. I decided to focus my energies on each area of my life, not just work.

2. Pay Attention to the Signposts of Good Health.

Sometimes we think we don't have time for healthier habits. But when I committed to using my early mornings hours for exercise, reading and spiritual growth, this became a time to recharge my mental batteries and refill my soul.

During the work day, I started making myself stop for at least thirty minutes to eat lunch away from my desk or other to-do's, ideally with members of our leadership team just to chat or talk about our day.

With the accountability of a colleague at school, I set a reasonable time to leave school each day. Or if I had to stay for an evening event, I found something to do not related to work in the time between.

I prioritized time with my family, even squeezing in mealtimes between games or activities with no phone or electronic devices allowed to interrupt it.

What steps can you take to maintain healthy habits that will influence the rest of your day? Small steps like nutrition, exercise, and rest will add much more meaning to your day, more time with you family, and a better attitude about working.

3. Personal Growth and Leadership Growth are not Separate Paths.

When you begin to prioritize the other important areas of life, ironically, you will find you are more effective in your performance at school.

When I invested in my personal growth as well as family time, I found I was more creative and optimistic at work. I found myself enjoying my colleagues more because of scheduled downtimes around lunches.

For instance, when our leadership team meets regularly around lunch, we inevitably talk more deeply or laugh more often. As a result, cooperative goal setting and action planning became more realistic when we take time to connect, not just react to the needs around us.

4. Rely on the Guidance of Your Personal Compass

I am a Christian, and my faith encourages me that if my greatest satisfaction is found in God, I also find my greatest satisfaction in life. This reminds me to keep the "hub" of my wheel of life centered correctly.

Let me encourage you to think deeply about the spiritual motivation in your life and behind your school leadership. Without an inner compass tuned to "true north," the journey is impossible to correctly navigate.

Wrap It Up

I still have days that wipe me out and seasons where life feels very unbalanced. But I have found my satisfaction with my work is intricately tied to my satisfaction in the other important areas of my life.

As you think about purpose-driven leadership, first take time to focus on the more meaningful parts of your life. You will be surprised how it encourages a more satisfying life as well as a more satisfying leadership journey.

Now It's Your Turn

What are some ways you have learned to balance work and downtime? What are some practical steps you can take to care for yourself so that your leadership stays effective?

Chapter 3

Focus On The Positive

—————— ~ ——————

Another important step in leadership is keeping your eye fixed on what matters most.

I had someone tell me once, "I would never want your job."

On the one hand, that may be true. Sometimes the negatives can be overwhelming.

When I was an assistant principal, for instance, I conducted hundreds of suspensions for drug/alcohol violations, fights, and weapon violations over the years.

In fact, it would be safe to say that I have administered thousands of other discipline actions for offenses like truancy, harassment, obscene language, driving violations, bus violations, theft, vandalism, computer hacking, and just about every other teen misbehavior you can imagine.

I am not alone.

As a principal, you will manage myriad of student and personnel issues, complaints, custody disputes, Facebook and texting drama that involve both students and parents at times.

You will counsel students wanting to drop out, those grieving over deceased parents, and ones afraid for their safety at school or at home.

Of course, your position also means scheduling your free time around supervising ball games, dances, concerts, contests, banquets, and fundraisers–all of this while trying to stay focused on the main purpose of school: educating students (not to mention being held responsible for their standardized test scores).

And the most difficult part of being a principal, of course, involves death. You will lose students to wrecks, illness, and suicide. And you will mourn the deaths of students, teachers, or their family members.

So, yes, some people would not want your job.

Why am I dwelling so much on the pressure of leadership?

Because that pressure is one reason we lose so many great leaders from our schools year after year.

Keeping Perspective

So how do we keep those pressures in perspective?

1. You must accept that negatives exist. They always will. This is the part of leadership that requires courage.
2. You must stay focused on the positives so they become what you celebrate at the end of each day.

Take-Away Story

For instance, the other day I did a walk-through my high school. During one class period, I saw Trigonometry students learning about inverse functions, computers students using Photoshop to build layered visual images, an Algebra I student demonstrating the solution to an equation on a Smart-board, FFA officers practicing speeches for upcoming state elections, English teachers co-teaching on avoiding plagiarism, chemistry students solving solution equations…all in just one hour of school!

When I think about the positives, I remember the years of last-second, cliffhanger victories (and defeats) at athletic events, impressive marching band routines, beautiful student art shows, FFA shows at county fairs, and rousing choral concerts.

You must never stop celebrating awesome student achievements, great teaching moments, creative ideas from team members, and successes of other school leaders.

Remember the spontaneous moments of hilarity with students and school colleagues.

Isn't it more satisfying to think about these positive moments multiplied over and over again every day rather than the difficulties?

Practical Action-Steps for Staying Positive

If like me, you sometimes wonder if school leadership is worth it, let me make some suggestions:

1. Get out of the office as much as possible and into classrooms where the most positive school energy is found.
2. Allow yourself to learn from the difficult moments and turn them into learning opportunities for yourself and others.
3. Treasure the time you have with the valuable students and staff in your school. It will go by faster than you think. And taking time to enjoy the small moments will help the difficult ones be more bearable.

Wrap It Up

Keeping the difficult moments in perspective can be like trying to view an optical illusion. It is easy to get overwhelmed by the incredible mix of colors, but when held in contrast to the positive reliefs, it is easier to see the beauty of it all.

It doesn't mean ignoring the negatives. It just means keeping them in perspective.

Now it's your Turn

What are some other suggestions you have for keeping a positive perspective while being a school leader? What are some of the better moments that help you keep perspective during the difficult time?

Chapter 4

Motivation by Wonder and Purpose

———————⌒———————

B efore I move on from the importance of purpose, I want to share with a conversation I had from a good friend and fellow school leader Lydia, an elementary principal, who wrote a compelling email to me.

Her thoughts are a good reminder of the deep satisfaction that comes when we have the right motives for school leadership. She wrote:

Ultimately, there is no satisfaction in work if there is no balance in life. It does not mean that I don't still experience heart-wrenching moments in this job, infuriating frustrations, or great losses filled with sadness.

I do believe those are part of our beautifully complicated existence in this world. Just today I had a teacher of tremendously strong faith find that she is cancer-free.

A child who read to me who has NOT been able to read through any of our instructional efforts thus far, but in the late part of his 2nd grade year, he has now read "Dan, the Tan Man" on his own.

And this morning I cried in a classroom where four children who are nonverbal and severely disabled TOOK TURNS in group time to work at the smart-board. My background was to work with some kids (and adults) like them.....and I know that God has graced me with an extreme privilege.

I've had quiet moments of connection with those who do not celebrate their successes in the ways most children do. I have truly felt that divine spirit settle over me in those privileged moments – much the way it feels to hold a new baby and KNOW God.

Like Lydia, I am trying to learn that healthy motivation not only changes leadership, it changes learning.

Have you ever thought of how learning is affected by motivation?

Imagine if a student is so overwhelmed by the wonder of a subject (whether it is Shakespeare or geometry or welding), that he or she pursues the subject for the love of understanding or mastering the subject.

Motivation by wonder is what separates a worker from a creator. It is why Benjamin Franklin helped pioneer new inventions and a new nation; it is why Einstein revolutionized the world of physics; it is why Steve Jobs developed Apple products.

It is what turns a job into a calling.

Be Aware of Counterproductive Motivations

I heard a lesson from one of my favorite writers and teacher, Timothy Keller, where he explained that people are often motivated by the two extremes: *fear* or *pride*.

Neither is healthy.

Fear motivates someone to take on a new challenge because he or she is afraid of the options; it motivates us to react to the moment or to over-react to what others think about us.

Pride, on the other hand, is another unhealthy motivation that often leads to burnout. Pride often pushes us by appealing to our egos. We expect perfection and don't allow failure to be part of the learning process.

When we are motivated by fear or pride, we push instead of pull others along.

Better Alternatives

So what is a third alternative to motivation by fear or pride? Keller says there are two alternatives: *beauty* and *duty*.

To put it simply, the most positive motivation is when you pursue a goal for the sheer joy or delight in pursuing and accomplishing the goal (beauty). Or when you pursue a path because you know it is the right thing to do (duty).

I like to think of these terms as *wonder* and *purpose*.

When you walk to your school each morning, remind yourself that you have the opportunity to make a difference. Remind yourself of the wonder and purpose behind your job.

Wrap It Up

When you focus on the deeper meaning of what you do, it helps you view students as people, not projects; parents as partners, not opponents; and teachers as team-members, not employees.

When we approach life motivated by wonder and purpose, you begin to see how it changes the way you lead and learn.

Now It's Your Turn

What motivations drive you to do your best work? How can you learn to keep a positive perspective even a midst the more mundane tasks of the day? What are some ways you can stay motivated to lead and learn today?

Chapter 5

Making Each Day Count

———————~———————

In *20,000 Days and Counting*,[6] Robert D. Smith explains the epiphany he had at 55 years of age when he calculated his years and realized he had lived 20,000 days. In his book, he shares the lessons he has learned along the journey and encourages others to make the most of their time.

During enrollment last year, I addressed a group of 8th graders who would be attending our school. I reminded them that at the high school level, most of them begin their journey here at age 14, having lived approximately 5,000 days.

---

6 Smith, Robert D. *20,000 Days and Counting: The Crash Course for Mastering Your Life Right Now*. Nashville, TN: Thomas Nelson, 2012. Print.

By the time they reach 6,500 days or 18 years old, they will graduate from high school—1,500 days to make some of the most important choices that will affect the rest of their lives!

Toward the end of last year, I was talking to a friend who is about twenty years younger than I am; he is experiencing the thrill of building his own business and raising a family. I was talking about life goals I had set for myself at his age.

He then asked me a sensible question that I wasn't ready for. "So what are your life goals now?"

I found myself stumbling around for an answer, when I finally admitted, "Mostly, I am just trying to survive."

That conversation haunted me for a while.

At the start of the year, I had the opportunity to spend a weekend in solitude, reflection and prayer. I came face-to-face with the realization of how unfocused my goals were for my work, my family, and myself.

So I began writing down new goals for my coming year. These were more than New Year resolutions. They were specific, measurable, written goals. Educators call these SMART goals.

I sat down with my wife and children and shared my goals with them and asked for their input and accountability on our goals as a family.

Like a boat that drifts away when not navigated properly or anchored securely, sometimes we find ourselves simply being pushed along by the current of life's circumstances.

At other times, survival is inevitable when we are struck by circumstances beyond our control.

Regardless of our circumstances, like Robert Smith, we must see that our days are numbered. Each day is a gift. What are the best ways we can encourage those around us and ourselves to make the most of our time?

As a school leader, you will learn that the goals you set will drive the focus of your entire school. So, here are three tips about goal setting to keep in mind:

1. Set Bold Personal Goals .

When is the last time you set specific, measurable goals for yourself and your team? Don't settle for easily attainable ones either.

Set bold, audacious goals. If you don't reach them, just remember at least you have reached higher than you would have with easy goals or no goals at all.

Where do want to see personal growth for yourself by the end of this year? Think through your goals for your family, career, your physical and spiritual health. What are ways to pursue your dreams and passions?

Where do you want to see your students, teachers, and leadership team grow by the end of this year?

Write them down and find someone to share them with so you have accountability in the journey. It is a lot easier to ask others to push themselves beyond their comfort zone when you are willing to do the same.

2. Model Making the Most of Each Day .

When others see us maximizing opportunities, not wasting time, doing excellent work, and enjoying your interactions, you set an example of making the most of each day.

To be really practical, when you are punctual, dress professionally, keep your commitments, avoid working on personal to-do's during school hours, walk hallways during passing periods, keep your promises—in all these actions, you are setting an example of what you hope to see in those around you.

3. Share Your Failures and Successes.

Sharing the ways you have learned from both failure and success gives others a good perspective on their own choices.

For instance, sometimes I will share with struggling students how I failed Algebra I when I was a ninth grader and then made an A+ when I took it the second time. I share with them the lessons I learned about self-discipline and time management.

When I talk to aspiring school leaders, for example, I am quick to explain the mistakes I have made with the hopes they can avoid the same pitfalls. It is embarrassing to admit our failures, but we also want to demonstrate how others can learn from them as well as their own.

Wrap It Up

Perhaps you've already surpassed the 20,000 days milestone, or maybe you're much earlier in the journey. Regardless of the count, each year is a new beginning.

Refuse to give in to drifting along or just surviving. Set goals for yourself that will maximize the countdown for yourself and for those around you.

Now It's Your Turn

What are some bold, audacious, measurable goals you have set for yourself? What are goals are you setting for your students, the team you lead, or those whom you love?

———～———

Part 2
Action Steps

———～———

Chapter 6

Better Managing Requests

---~---

Now that we have explored the importance of motivation, let's discuss some of the other nuts-and-bolts of school leadership.

My first year as a school administrator, I began as an assistant principal in a school of 1,300 high school students. I was convinced I would not repeat some of the frustrating habits of my former leaders.

Specifically, I wanted to be a leader who consistently followed through on requests from teachers. What I didn't anticipate was how many requests I would receive in a day.

Before long I realized it was virtually impossible to respond to the number of "fires" that came up daily. After much trial and error, I finally began to settle on how to prioritize so many competing demands. I also began to understand why some of my predecessors had a difficult time with follow-through.

In the process, I discovered some truths that may help you in better managing requests:

1. Give up Your 'Savior' Complex

Don't make the mistake of thinking you can find the solution to every problem in your building. During my first year, in a typical hour as I walked through hallways and classrooms, I would often be stopped two or three times with requests. I would write down each request on a legal pad I carried with me.

By the end of the day, I had pages of notes. Then I would sit down that evening or the next morning to follow-up on them.

Bad idea.

What I discovered was that my list grew every day. I found myself spending hours of work just on follow-up requests. What I didn't know then was how poorly I was modeling leadership for my teachers. As a leader, I still needed to be consistent in communicating back to my teachers and staff.

But my system of was not helping me prioritize nor was I teaching them how to become problem solvers.

I was also constantly "putting out fires" instead of focusing on goals for what was most important for our school. Something had to change, and it began when I admitted I was not the end-all for every problem.

2. If It's Important, Have Them Write It Down

It took me a long time to learn, but eventually I decided on some more practical steps.

First, I stopped carrying a legal pad. When a team member stopped me with a concern or request, I would first decide if this was something I could coach them to handle on their own. I could tell them who to see for resources or how to talk to a parent about a struggling student, etc.

Sometimes I needed to provide immediate follow-up or

support. If that was the case, I needed to help find a solution; that is my responsibility.

But if they brought me an issue that might take further consideration and was not an immediate need, I would say, "Thank you for letting me know that. If that is important to you, please follow up to me with an email about it."

Sometimes just listening to others is what they really want. In my case, I coach my teammates to email me if the situation or issue is still a priority to them after our conversation.

On the one hand, we often find solutions in the moment. On the other hand, I found my to-do list of follow-ups decreasing through these steps.

3. Learn To Teach Others How to Find Their Own Solutions

I don't think I can overemphasize the importance of delegation. Here are a couple of analogies I have heard about learning to delegate or coach other to find their own solutions:

One, a coach never puts on the helmet and pads to

jump in the game for his players. He coaches them. School leaders must do the same; it is not our job to jump into every crisis and create a solution; it is more important to train and coach your team members into becoming problem solvers.

Another analogy is one I have heard called the "monkey on the shoulder" practice. When someone comes to you with a problem that jumps off his/her shoulders onto yours, expect the person to become a part of the solution.

Make sure he takes his monkey with him when he leaves.

Wrap It Up

As a high school principal, I find myself learning many of these lessons again and again. Prioritizing time and requests is ultimately about creating a school climate where student are served well. If we are unable to manage our time, students will ultimately be the ones who suffer the consequences.

To better manage requests, give up your savior complex, encourage others to write down their requests, and learn to help others find their own solutions where possible. In the end, your teachers and students will reap the benefits.

Now It's Your Turn

What are some ways you have learned to manage time or requests? Do you have a favorite resource for time management? Start planning now some strategies for how you will manage multiple requests.

Chapter 7

Dealing with Difficult People

———————— ∼ ————————

One of your most important jobs as a school leader will be to navigate through the paths of difficulties.

It my seem a sad reality, but you will never stop encountering people who are difficult or challenging. Earlier this year, I had a mother pointing her finger in my face and yelling so loudly that she was spitting. It was unpleasant to say the least.

If you are like me, you want school leadership to be about inspiring or encouraging others to reach shared goals. In reality, leadership also requires managing complicated situations or people.

Over the years, I have begun to learn practical skills in

dealing with people who are upset, angry, or just plain mean.

I don't always do it correctly, but I believe with practice, anyone can learn to maximize the potential of finding solutions in conflicts.

Whether you face challenging people on a daily basis, or only occasionally, here are some tips I have learned from my own experience as well as watching others who consistently manage difficult people:

1. Make sure you are not the difficult person.

Most of us don't like to admit it, but often our own attitude, demeanor, and level of patience significantly affect the way we interact with someone in a difficult moment.

When someone comes to see you in the midst of a highly emotional situation, whether they are distressed about their own situation or someone else's, they are often anticipating resistance. So, the first thing you should convey in those situations is an open, welcome, and listening attitude.

Instead of immediately going on the offensive or defensive, try to let them know you are pleased to see them and want to help.

Also, try to gauge your own temperament. In the school setting, it is not uncommon to immediately go from one high stress situation to another. Try to remind yourself that the person you are encountering has not seen your whole day—just the very moment you are in.

Likewise, you have not seen his or her whole day either. By keeping in mind that you need to not be the difficult one, you are more likely to really listen and often decrease some of the heightened emotions involved in the difficult situation.

2. Seek to understand before being understood.

Stephen Covey teaches this principle in his 7 Habits for Highly Successful People.[7]

Don't assume the best communication is when you're the only one speaking. When someone comes to you with a

---

7 Covey, Stephen R. *The 7 Habits of Highly Effective People: Restoring the Character Ethic.* New York: Free, 2004. Print.

difficulty or problem or even with a confrontation, if your goal is to find a solution, you first have to understand the problem.

One practical tip I learned from my mentors has been to take notes when someone is sharing concerns. First, this helps you keep the thoughts and the details they are sharing in front of you so that you can separate the facts from the emotions.

Second, taking notes demonstrates to the other party that you take their concerns seriously. Many times, when people feel confident that the problem is being taken seriously, a difficult meeting can turn into a bridge-building opportunity.

Sometimes understanding requires some coaching. I worked with a great assistant principal who would say, "I'm having a hard time understanding. Help me see the video in my head of what you are talking about." This was a great way to give the person permission to calm down, be specific, and feel understood. Good problem solving happens not only with a good picture of the situation but also when you have set the right tone for the conversation.

3. Be firm but friendly.

Granted, there are times when a difficult person completely misunderstands the facts. And bluntness is not always off the table.

So don't be afraid to tell the truth with kindness. When you do, you will gain the respect of the listener much more than excuses or non-committal statements.

A good example of this was a fellow administrator I knew who lost her temper and yelled at a student who was skipping classes. The boy's mother came to the school very upset that her child was being disciplined and that the administrator had yelled at the student. When the parent confronted her, she simply told the truth.

"Yes, Mrs. Smith, I did yell," she said. "I found your son in the hallway trying to sneak into the gym after I had just confronted him ten minutes earlier for loitering in the halls and had told him to be punctual with getting to class. When I saw him the second time, I yelled at him like I would my own child for being disrespectful of our time and wasting his own. That's when I escorted him to the office and called you."

The mother's countenance softened, she sighed, and to my friend's surprise, she said, "Can you help me learn how to deal with him? He never does what I tell him to do at home."

Obviously, I am not advocating yelling at students, but my friend's polite frankness turned a potentially volatile situation into a learning moment for everyone involved.

4. Change your posture or use humor when appropriate.

You will be amazed how disarming it can be to an angry person when they are greeted with a smile and a handshake.

Sometimes sitting at your desk is appropriate for a meeting, but at other times, I like to come out from around my desk and sit together at a table or in matching chairs to speak to someone.

Closed fists or crossed arms convey anxiety or frustration, so I consciously maintain an open posture with relaxed hands on my knees or desk, or I take notes while pausing to make good eye contact. All of these mannerisms convey that we are not enemies but allies.

Even when you are explaining or conveying information that is hard for someone else to hear, it is often much easier for them to accept it when your body language conveys you are relaxed, not attacking.

I also find strong words are more effectively delivered in a calm voice. Will you always do this well? No. But try to purposely practice these postures in order to create the best setting for a good conversation.

Also, if appropriate, find something in the situation that you can eventually laugh about. With students, that is not difficult—they provide lots of good content for humor!

5. Agree to disagree.

So, what do you do when you have tried all of the above, but the other person is still upset or disagrees with you? Remember the goal is about what is best for everyone involved.

It is not about winning or losing.

If someone has a reason for still disagreeing or being unsatisfied, give him or her specific instructions for how to appeal that concern to someone else in the leadership structure.

Even if it's a matter that goes nowhere else after the immediate conversation, sometimes it just helps to say, "You know. We're just going to have to agree to disagree. " You're not ending the conversation by saying, "I'm right. You're wrong." You may not even be changing a decision, but you are demonstrating the desire for mutual respect even in the midst of a disagreement.

Remember in the business of school, you will most likely encounter this person again in the community, at a ball game, or maybe even at church.

You want to be able to look them in the eye and know that you still treated them with the dignity you would want someone to show you in a disagreement.

6. Consider Bringing All Parties to the Table.

Sometimes, resolving conflicts requires more than just a one-on-one conversation. If the conflict involves multiple parties, bringing them all to the table helps shed light on the situation and makes it easier to cut through misunderstandings and reach solutions.

Learning how to resolve conflicts among parties could be a whole post by itself, so I will save that for another time.

Wrap It Up

At the end of the day, none of us likes confrontation or difficult moments. Most people are prone to fight or flight. But there is another option.

By checking your own motives, seeking to understand, remaining firm and friendly, maintaining an open posture, sometimes agreeing to disagree, or bringing all parties to the table, you can go a long way in turning difficult conversations into more positive outcomes.

Now It's Your Turn

Can you think of a time you were able to diffuse a tense situation or person? What steps did you use? What could you add to the list above? What are some great resources you recommend for someone who wants to learn how to better communicate in difficult situations?

Chapter 8

Showing Appreciation for Teachers

—————— ～ ——————

J ust as important as it is to deal effectively with difficult moments, it is equally important to lead through service and support.

As you lead your school, you can never do so without a fabulous team. And one of your jobs as a leader is to motivate, inspire, and support them.

A friend once told me, "One good deed is worth more than a thousand good intentions." You can never overestimate the power of showing appreciation.

Sometimes I am guilty of good intentions without good actions. But when it comes to appreciating others, my good intentions won't ever let others know they're appreciated as much as a few simple actions.

Simple and creative acts of appreciation go a long way in an occupation where monetary bonuses and pay raises aren't something to which you have access or directly control.

Here are some ideas you can employ throughout the school year to let others know they are appreciated for their hard work:

1. Send "Kudos" Emails.

As I walk through our building, one of my favorite activities is to take notes on what I see students and teachers doing. Afterwards, it is fun to email the entire staff a message titled "kudos."

Here's an example of one I've sent out:

"Teachers, This morning I observed students identifying the tools and small-engine parts in Ag Mechanics, solving recursive equations in Trig, drawing periodic tables in Physical Science, conversing

with new vocabulary in Spanish I, and converting milligram measurements in Marine Biology. Others were taking quizzes, reading aloud, or learning with SMART boards. There is a reason our school-wide scores continue to improve; you are teaching well! Keep up the good work!"

2. Create a Video Montage.

An idea I borrowed from another principal this year was creating a short "Way to Go!" video clip for teachers. Using the built-in camera on my iPad, I discretely caught teachers in action.

After emailing each clip to myself and using Windows Live Movie Maker, it took about 25 minutes after school editing the clips into a short presentation. After uploading it to Youtube, I was able to send the link via email.

When I shared it, I reminded our teachers that this was just a sample of the rock-star teaching they do on a daily basis.

3. Hand-Written Notes or Cards.

Sometimes a hand-written card or short note says 'thank you' best. The first year I did this, I had more than one veteran teacher tell me they couldn't remember ever receiving a hand-written thank-you from a school administrator.

Words of affirmation are motivational. I usually keep notes others have given me. It is encouraging to pull them out occasionally and remind myself why I chose to be an educator. If I love those notes, I have to remember others do too.

4. Monthly Awards.

It is a tradition at our school to consistently recognize one or more team members a month for their service to students or the school community. We like to announce and present our teachers-of-the-month at faculty meetings.

Certificates and gift-cards are simple gestures, but these awards also provide a platform for encouraging all of us to maximize their time helping students and one another.

It is easy to "become an island" when you are teaching. Acknowledging one person's great job affirms what great learning is taking place throughout the entire school.

5. Newsletter/Website Publicity.

Each time we have a significant success, we like to let others know by publishing a quick note and photo in our school newsletter. Many of those stories also appear on the school website.

In addition, our superintendent is a great cheerleader; he will often send notices to the entire district via email of teacher and student achievements.

We also forward those notices on to our local newspaper, where many of them end up reported to the entire community.

6. Face-to-Face

Nothing replaces the times when you can look someone straight in the eye and tell him or her how much you appreciate him or her. Sometimes this happens spontaneously when you have a moment in a hallway or catch someone on a planning period or at lunch.

Of course, a great time to do this is during evaluation meetings. If you value meaningful feedback, you can be sure the people on your team value the feedback as well.

7. Food, Food, Food!

Whether it's doughnuts for meetings, potluck lunches, free dinners during parent conferences, or an occasional meal out-together with a team member, everyone appreciates something tasty.

We have the privilege of having some folks on our team who love to cook. Instead of catering-in or doing a potluck for a recent appreciation luncheon, we bought what was needed for our in-house chefs to create some of their favorite dishes. It was a tremendous success.

We also like to start our school year off by hosting a lunch with our newest teachers to match them with mentor team members. At the district level, we have a long tradition of beginning the first district-wide meeting of the year with a barbecue lunch.

Wrap It Up

If I had the ability to pass out real bonuses or pay commission to my team members, I would be thrilled. Even if I could, I would still want to show them appreciation

through emails, catching them on camera, little notes, monthly awards, newsletter/website publications, face-to-face conversations and meals, cakes and treats.

Each year we gear up for Teacher Appreciation Week, and we'll do some great meals and small gifts, etc. But we can't forget that great team members deserve thanks every week of the year.

Now It's Your Turn

What are some ways you have found to show appreciation for your team members? What are some ways you most enjoy being appreciated for a job well done? Think of one way you can celebrate someone today, and then do it.

Chapter 9

Disciplining with Dignity

———————～———————

No doubt the job of a principal is to set the tone for the behavior expected school-wide, and school discipline is often a hotly debated topic of discussion.

If viewed simply as punishment, it is often ineffective in changing behavior. But if viewed as a way to measure, check, and coach, the results are often more positive.

A Quick Story

Toward the end of school this year, I had a situation with a student that involved some out-of-school discipline. A couple of days after the meeting, one of my teachers stopped me in the hallway.

She told me that the boy's mother had confided in her

that at a prior district her child had been in trouble before.

The mother said that this time, she was pleased with the outcome. The way she put it was, "I have never been treated with so much dignity."

That statement caught me off guard.

I thought back to how we handled his discipline. All I could think of was how I tried to treat them like I would want to be treated if the tables were turned.

With that in mind, I began to think about how we manage discipline at our school and wanted to share eight ways students can be disciplined with dignity:

1. Set high expectations .

Before school begins each year, we hold a freshman orientation meeting for students and parents. It gives us an opportunity to welcome them and explain what our expectations are for their time in high school.

We introduce them to our leadership team, school sponsors, and representatives from other organizations like

Career Technology or other recruiters. After school is in session, our leadership team visits every English class to pass out student handbooks.

These classroom meetings usually take at a week to complete, but they are so worth it. By the end, we have had face-to-face interaction with every student. They also sign that they have received and understand the expectations for the year.

2. Let the consequence fit the infraction.

In addition to expected behaviors, in your student handbook, you should decide and publish ahead of time what are common responses to expected misbehaviors. We have pre-set actions set for infractions like skipping, tardies, disruptive behavior, etc.

Here's a common rule of thumb: As the infraction increases in threat to school or student safety, so does the discipline action response.

For instance, any student who commits an act that is

either criminal or violent can expect the most severe of consequences.

On the other hand, a student who is late to class is disciplined appropriately but never like a student who hurts or injures someone else.

The bottom line: Use common sense in the discipline you choose.

3. Be consistent.

One of the worst lessons you can teach students is that there are no consequences for wrong choices.

When you decide ahead of time what are the common discipline actions for an offense, it makes it easier to assign them consistently from student to student.

Discipline must be firm, fair, and consistent if you are going to create an atmosphere of safe learning.

4. Be creative when necessary.

Occasionally, I work with students who may not have the

same resources as all other students. For instance, some kids don't have a way home other than the bus. Thankfully, that is rare in my school, but if I am working with a student who is unable to attend an after school detention, for instance, perhaps I can let him/her opt for some lunchroom or campus cleanup time. Or his parents may prefer I assign him time in our In-School Placement room instead.

The point is that being consistent doesn't always mean every student ends up in the same discipline assignment.

Don't be afraid to be creative when necessary. Offering different but equal-in-time choices also help put the final decision in the student or parent's hand, which can be both empowering and helpful.

5. Be polite.

I try to make it a habit to welcome students when I call them to my office. Often I will greet them with a handshake or a 'how are you doing today?' exchange.

Especially in situations where I know a student is going to receive serious discipline, I make a special effort to deliver the news in calm, polite terms.

Occasionally, I will confront a situation where I need to speak in stronger and clearer tones to a student. But I try to ask myself how I would want to receive this kind of talk if I were in his/her shoes.

A funny side note: Once after disciplining a girl for multiple cell phone violations, she visited her counselor afterwards to complain about me.

She said I smiled too much and seemed to be enjoying giving her discipline. She had tried to argue her way out of the discipline, and apparently, I smiled while telling her I wouldn't change my mind. One of my teachers heard about the incident and promptly sent me a photo-shop poster of myself with a huge Cheshire-cat smile on my face and the words "Service with a smile" blazoned across the poster.

6. Be Specific and Document.

When you administer discipline to a student, make sure there is documentation of the incident. If it is not recorded, it didn't happen.

When a student admits to a serious infraction, also have him/her put it in his or her own writing. When discipline involves out of school placement, parents should be provided documentation for signatures.

Documentation serves three purposes:

- It provides evidence of everything that is being discussed or decided in regards to a student.
- It provides you legal protection that you have not violated anyone's rights to due process.
- Most importantly, it makes it clear to all parties involved exactly what is expected for the student to be successful.

7. Serve and Teach.

Every situation can be an opportunity to serve and teach. Student discipline is an especially key time to try to assist parents or guardians in teaching strong life lessons to their children.

Whether that is coaching a student on how to raise grades, or connecting them with a good counselor, disciplining students is much more fulfilling if you are exploring ways to help students in the process.

The goal is not just to punish; the goal is to discipline, improve, and serve.

8. Communicate Trust.

I am honest with students that if they have violated my trust or the trust of their parents or teachers, they will only earn back that trust over time. And long-term patterns of doing what's right will earn trust back more than anything else.

I also try to let them know that I still like them and expect them to be successful. Even though I am holding them accountable and letting them suffer consequences, my end goal is to proudly watch them walk across that stage at graduation knowing they will have a great future.

Wrap It Up

Discipline is so much more than just assigning detentions, Saturday Schools, etc. Like a good classroom, school-wide discipline is greatly affected by relationships and rapport.

When students feel like you still like them even when having to correct them, they are so much more likely to work on improving their own behavior.

The same holds true in all relationships of life. I like to be shown dignity and respect, and it is my responsibility to model what I want to see in others.

Now It's Your Turn

Student discipline is both an art and science. What are some ways you have learned to discipline with dignity? What ideas would you add to this list? What are some new steps you can take to see the positive behaviors you would like to with your students?

—∽—

Part 3

Keeping Your Perspective

—∽—

Chapter 10

And Then I Met A Teacher

———————～———————

Principals must never stop being teachers. A good friend once told me he could think of many times when he has heard someone say, "And then he met a teacher, and it changed…"

I want to share two stories of men I talked to recently whose lives were changed by educators:

Story 1

Jim Wengo was fresh out of high school when he started working at the local butcher shop. But his high school agriculture teacher, John Krivokapish, had other plans for him.

When he heard of an area college work study program for those who could score well on a civil service exam, Mr.

Krivokapish walked into the butcher store and told Jim's boss he needed to borrow him for a couple of hours.

Removing the blood stained apron, Jim followed his teacher to the local college where he took an exam on the spot. That test resulted in Jim's opportunity to begin college.

He kept working as a butcher while he finished his degree. Then he was recruited into the Army where he served as an officer and engineer until his retirement. He traveled the world, raised a family, built his dream home, and now enjoys the benefits of a life of hard work and God's grace.

He met a teacher, and it changed everything.

Story 2

Dennis Queen had a difficult relationship with his father. When he dropped out of a high school, a local elementary school principal, Don Ross, drove over to his house and talked him into enrolling in summer school so he could have enough credits to graduate. Dennis joined the Marines.

After a four-year tour of duty, Dennis returned home. He hadn't communicated with Mr. Ross for four years. But his principal showed up again, drove him to a local college, and helped him enroll.

Dennis became a teacher, a pastor, and eventually a school superintendent. His life has been one of incredible service and positive influence in the lives of others.

He met an educator, and it changed everything.

These are both true stories told to me by men who have personally inspired me by their examples. I don't know how many times you've heard the same story. Sometimes it is a coach, a pastor, a relative or neighbor.

But they are all teachers—people like Mr. Krivokapish or Mr. Ross who are willing to invest their time in a younger person to encourage them to do something bigger, pursue a dream, take a step in the right direction.

In turn, people like Jim Wengo and Dennis Queen inspire others, including me. Now it's my turn. And it's your turn too.

Mentoring

Four years ago, we started a program at my school called Mentor 180. Each year we team new ninth graders with a volunteer teacher and an older student.

These teams meet weekly, and mentors provide direction, input, and listening ears to new high school students who may otherwise feel like they're on their own. As a result, we have seen great improvement in many young people who were formerly labeled "at risk".

Last year, we had one young lady who came to our school after she had failed the year before. Her teacher and student mentor met with her weekly to coach and encourage her. She finished her freshman year passing all her classes—five of them with A's!

She met a teacher and a mentor, and it changed

everything.

Wrap It Up

People do amazing things when they know someone who is willing to guide, direct, and influence them. Whether you are on the receiving end or the giving end in life, first take time to let your "influencers" know you appreciate them.

And then look around for someone who may just need to meet you.

Now It's Your Turn

Who were some of the "influencers" in your life? If possible, let them know they are appreciated. What are some other stories you know of people's lives changed when they met a teacher? What innovative ways is your school connecting with students who need mentoring?

Chapter 11
Sanity During Stressful Times

———— ~ ————

The spring that I transitioned from assistant principal to principal, I began to wonder if I had made the right decision.

As the school year closed, and my former principal departed, I found myself wrapping up many of my former responsibilities while simultaneously managing my new ones.

In essence, I found that in the short term, I would be doing two jobs at once.

Suddenly, my sense of control began to melt away as my list of "to do's" seemed to grow longer and longer. Eventually, I found myself in the same place I had nine years earlier as an assistant principal and ten years before that as a new teacher.

Frankly, my plate was full and I was beginning to feel overwhelmed.

Thankfully, I was able to remember that familiar feeling I had had before in new positions, and I reminded myself that stressful times are often a season. I was able to step away mentally from my situation and analyze some best approaches.

Do you ever find yourself in a place where you wonder how you will maintain your sanity during stressful times? If so, it may help you to consider and act on the following four helpful tips:

1. Maintain a sensible schedule (where you can).

Exercise and family time may not seem as important now as your many to-do's and deadlines, but ignoring these priorities will lead to less energy and loss of focus. I find that if I can still maintain some semblance of normality in a daily routine, my work seems more manageable.

Identify what habits you need to keep practicing even during stressful times. At the same time, it is okay to be forgiving of yourself during the hardest times and admit you cannot do it all.

During a stressful season, give yourself some grace and remember a more sensible time will come again.

2. Remember, you are not always in complete control.

This is hard for me, but stressful times are good reminders to me of my own infallibility. I am not ultimately in control of all my circumstances. It is good for me to rest in knowing I need God's help in every task of life.

The best part about school is that regardless of how long my to-do list becomes, I can't control the school calendar. Some things may be left undone, so stay focused on the ones that matter most. Separate what needs to be done from what may have to be left undone.

3. Maintain a To-do List .

I know it seems like a no-brainer, but sometimes your

overwhelming tasks are more easily managed when you write them down first, prioritize, and then mark them off as you accomplish them.

I have been using Workflowy.com as a way to do this better, and I love it!

4. Let others know you need help.

As I heard someone once say, "You are not Superman, so tuck in your cape and ask for help." If you work in a school or on a team, you must realize that incredible people are around you who could also help. I found sharing my schedule with co-workers allowed them to give me feedback on ways I could better tackle issues.

It also gave us the ability to discuss how to work together on some of tasks we could share.

Don't be afraid to ask for help. Leaders who fail to delegate usually fail to accomplish their most important goals and eventually burn out.

5. Keep Your Work Load In Perspective .

I touched on this point before, but I want to reiterate that seasons of hard work are usually seasons. I remember once in college when I worked on a landscape crew.

We showed up on a work site one day where we had been asked to clear a 5-acre lot of leaves. Trees surrounded the entire property and all we had were rakes, a mower, and a trailer.

At first, I turned to other college friend in charge of the job and said, "I don't think we can do this."

He replied, "We can't if we don't get to work."

Thankfully, our crew of hard working guys was also creative. Soon we started using a mower to blow leaves, blankets to transport the leaves away, and we raked and raked all day. We finished the job.

Lesson learned? You never finish a job until you start, and you often accomplish it one rake full at a time.

Wrap It Up

If you find yourself overwhelmed by work, please

remember you are not alone. And remember not all stress is bad stress. But don't be overwhelmed. Remember to

keep a sensible schedule where you can, give yourself grace, share your workload when possible, and accomplish your goals one task at a time. And when it is all said and done, don't forget to celebrate!

Now It's Your Turn

What are some ways you find to hold on to perspective during stressful times? How do you manage your to-dos so that you can accomplish goals without feeling overwhelmed?

Chapter 12

Lessons from *Seabiscuit*

———— ❧ ————

Laura Hillenbrand's *Seabiscuit*[8] is a biography about a famous racehorse made even more famous by film version. The biography centers on the lives of three men whom *Seabiscuit* involves in a network of drama, suspense, defeat, and triumph.

Not only is the story mesmerizing, but also it contains many life lessons for school leaders or anyone interested in personal growth or improvement for their team, school, or organization.

Here are ten lessons I pulled from the story that apply to school leadership:

---

[8] *Hillenbrand, Laura. Seabiscuit: An American Legend. New York: Ballantine, 2002. Print.*

1. People accomplish amazing feats when they are unified around a common cause.

The story's main characters couldn't have been more different in background, upbringing, and temperament: Seabiscuit's owner Charles Howard, a wealthy entrepreneur; Trainer Tom Smith, a lonely cowboy from the plains; and jockey Red Pollard, a former-boxer-turned-rider.

When their paths crossed directly on a horse Smith chose on a whim, these men became a band of brothers who each played a part in the horse's success.

Lesson: People who bring different strengths or weaknesses to the table may surround you. But when you are unified around a common vision, you can accomplish the unbelievable.

2. Sometimes your most unlikely prospects can become your greatest assets.

Seabiscuit was not sleek racehorse. No one expected a

horse of his shape to run fast. Likewise, Jockey Red Pollard was down on his luck, overworked, and malnourished when he happened upon the horse right after Howard had purchased him. In addition, Smith, the silent cowboy trainer, recognized the kindred spirits in Pollard and Seabiscuit. He decided to convince Howard to take a chance on all of them.

These relatively unknown characters came together to form a team that surprised the world with their racehorse that could out-run others by lengths.

Lesson: No matter how difficult the background, you can still surprise yourself and others with success.

3. Success requires risk.

Of course the sport of racing is always a gamble. But any grand achievement almost always requires some risk. For Howard, Smith, and Pollard, this meant calculated risk. They knew the best weather and ground conditions for Seabiscuit. They carefully trained him for races based on those conditions, but they sometimes took chances on the running in the worst conditions just to have a shot at winning.

Lesson: When you know your environment, your strengths and weaknesses, and where your greatest returns may occur, then you can make calculated risks that may lead to great victories.

4. Loyalty and trust are the hallmark of winning teams.

Each man on Seabiscuit's team knew how to trust the others' strengths. One time before an important race, Smith the trainer had a hunch something was wrong with Seabiscuit. He had no physical evidence, but he could sense the horse was possibly wounded.. Tragedy struck when these signs were ignored.

Howard the owner had the same instinct for knowing how to work publicity to his horse's favor, and Smith knew that Howard, as owner, was ultimately in control.

While the other men worked their strengths, Pollard the jockey understood the ride of the horse better than anyone.

His ability to read Seabiscuit in the moment of "battle" allowed him to ride him to victory after victory.

Lesson: As you learn and rely on the strengths of those around you, rest in your roles, and trust one another's instincts, you develop into a winning team.

5. Believing and acting on dreams will separate fantasy from reality.

Victory always follows action. And action is the result of imagination, creativity, planning, and execution. As Howard's team dreamed of winning, they took all the right steps to train well, to practice wisely, and to compete with cleverness. Seabiscuit embodied the same competiveness by nature.

Lesson: Don't be afraid to dream. As long as you follow dreams with wise action, you are poised for turning ideas into accomplishments.

6. Publicity is a great tool for motivating support for your cause.

Seabiscuit became a national sensation not only because he was a winner but also because Howard befriended the press, let them participate in his successes, and allowed enough distance between them and his racehorse to keep them hungry for more.

Lesson: Publicity is a great way to celebrate success and allow others to celebrate with you. It often opens the door to other opportunities.

7. Losing a battle doesn't mean you have lost the war.

Seabiscuit was not without his grueling defeats. Jockey Red Pollard experienced so many injuries, he had to be replaced more than once while he recovered. Seabiscuit knew the pain of being outrun, the agony of injury, and the difficult path of rehabilitation.

But the team was able to keep their eye on the ultimate goal of reaching the next level.

Lesson: Defeat does not ultimately equal the end. It is a natural result of trying, risking, and reaching for new levels.

8. Sometimes your greatest defeats become your greatest opportunities.

It is likely Seabiscuit would have never achieved as much as he did had he won in some of his earliest big races. The lessons learned through defeat taught his team how to re-train toward Seabiscuit's strengths.

Lesson: Open doors often result directly after a seeming defeat. Don't forget to look for the opportunities that rise from being knocked down.

9. Success is contagious.

As one of the most famous athletes in the world, Seabiscuit became the emblem of underdog hero for the American audience.

Thousands greeted him as he traveled cross-country via train. Tens of thousands overwhelmed stadiums to see him run. Millions flocked around radios to hear of his racing progress.

Lesson: Success breeds success. Remember to celebrate

the small victories; they tend to lead to the larger ones.

10. Legacies are built over time, not just in one moment.

The nation's love for Seabiscuit did not happen over night. Unlike most racehorses, Seabiscuit had many years of racing before retirement.

He epitomized the same struggle for survival that many of his Great Depression fans felt during trying times. When the horse was retired, people still came to visit to take photos and they followed the races of his offspring.

Lesson: A good name endures much longer if its possessor shows long-term reliability and dependability. No flash-in-the-pan winner builds a legacy as strong as a consistent one.

Wrap It Up

Seabiscuit was not only an amazing horse. He also connected the lives of unlikely individuals into a cohesive force of unified vision and execution—a team willing to take risks, to trust one another, to act on their dreams, to rally others to their support, to turn losses into opportunities, to celebrate their successes, and to build a legacy.

As you lead your school or take on your next big adventure, don't forget the lessons you can learn from history—even the ones from a racehorse. Let's rally our students and teams around a unified commitment to blaze new paths together.

Now It's Your Turn

What are some of your favorite books or true stories that yield lessons for leadership? In what ways can you learn to value the differences among your own team members in order to unify around a common goal?

Chapter 13

Leaning On Other People's Expertise

———⌇———

A few months into one school year, I was planning to attend a principal association meeting near the state capital.

Since I was going alone, I asked a principal friend from a neighboring district if we could ride together. Little did I know how much I would be learning on that ride.

We spent the time there and back sharing insights and stories from our schools. It was such a great conversation that I opened my iPad and starting taking notes.

Sometimes our greatest resource for change is as close as a phone call (or a car ride in this case). As I thought about that conversation, I reflected on other ways I have learned from simply asking.

Do you ever think about areas in your work or life where you wish you had more insight?

Here are four examples of ways to reach out to others to learn from their expertise:

1. Connect with other people on your team or in your field.

I am blessed to share leadership with some incredible individuals in my school and district. Bouncing ideas off them always leads to better decisions. So look around at your colleagues. They have great ideas and have the context of working closely with you to give you advice no one else can.

In addition to my own team, I have learned from many others. Last year, I had the privilege of sitting on the interview committee for State Assistant Principal.

It was a beneficial opportunity to spend the day

gleaning great ideas from some incredible administrators.

You don't have to be on an interview committee to have the chance to talk to great leaders. Pick up the phone, send an email, or ask someone to lunch.

Being a part of a principal's association allows me to connect and learn from other leaders across the state and nation.

I have also discovered the power of sharing ideas via Twitter. The years are over of the principal being a leader alone on an island. If you are willing to reach out, you can learn so much from one another.

2. Visit Successful Schools or Organizations.

One of my favorite learning experiences is spending time at other schools. Last year, I was able to visit neighboring schools known for their incredible student test scores.

We took a team of from our school and spent the morning observing their teachers working on data teams during their planning periods.

We also sat together with their teachers and administrators to discuss strategies and learn from their experiences.

It is chore to leave your building for a day, but it is also great to come back with new perspectives and ideas that you can use to see your own improvement.

Our opportunity happened via email exchanges and text messages with administrators there. You can do the same in reaching out to an organization you would really like to visit.

In addition to schools, I enjoy getting to know business professionals. Finding out how they run their businesses or companies gives me more contexts for coaching students on careers.

Visiting businesses also helps me understand better processes for some of the management and "customer service" side of school.

3. Contact Outside Experts.

Over the years, our district often invites law enforcement and emergency officials to touch base with us, stay familiar with our buildings, and advise us on areas of concern. Your local emergency responders should be your best allies in this area.

Our district has the privilege of having our own Student Resource Officer. Through his leadership, we have been able to obtain grants for improved camera installations.

He has also brought workshops on school safety to our principals from the Oklahoma Office of Homeland Security. You may be amazed at the free seminars available to you if you just ask.

In the summer before my first year as principal, I invited our local fire marshal to walk through our school with me. It was a good time to revisit our tornado procedures in order to make sure our plans were in line with lessons learned in the most recent tornado tragedies from the previous spring.

I am glad I asked.

We were able to identify some areas that needed changing and will be implementing those changes with the new school year.

Building relationships with local emergency responders is also a great way to keep ties strong for the next situation you may be working together.

The same applies to curriculum, technology, or athletics—experts in those fields make resources from whom you can learn.

4. Learn From Books, Conferences, Podcasts.

Sometimes our most obvious go-to's are right at our finger tips. Here a few great reads that have been recommended to me by school leaders:

Great to Good by Jim Collins

Nice Bike—Making Meaningful Connections on the Road of Life by Mark Scharenbroich

The 21 Irrefutable Laws of Leadership: Follow Them and People Will Follow You by John C. Maxwell

For a longer list of books recommended by school leaders, you can visit this link: http://astore.amazon.com/williamdparke-20

The same is true of attending conferences or listening to podcasts. One of my favorite leadership podcasts is Michael Hyatt's *This Is Your Life* (http://michaelhyatt.com/thisisyourlife). As the former CEO of Nelson Publishing, he provides practical, hands-on advice for others in leadership.

Wrap It Up

Seeking counsel from others ensures greater possibility of success in any endeavor. Pick up the phone, send an email, or just go visit other leaders. Read books, listen to podcasts, or attend conferences. You may be surprised the new ideas and opportunities these resources may open for you and your team.

Now It's Your Turn

Who are some go-to's you have found valuable for your

school or team? What are some experiences or resources you have found helpful that you can share with others?

Chapter 14

The Rise of Theodore Roosevelt

———————— ~ ————————

A nother example of leadership learned from good books is Edmund Morris's, *The Rise of Theodore Roosevelt.*[9] In it he chronicles Roosevelt's life from birth to the day he becomes President. It is another great story that teaches lessons about school leadership, both good and bad.

At nearly 800 pages of detailed narrative, Morris paints the picture of a boy who began life frail and sickly, developed his mind and imagination through reading and travel, beat all odds through intense self-improvement, and lived a life of eagerness to fight at every opportunity.

———————————————

[9] *Morris, Edmund. The Rise of Theodore Roosevelt. New York: Ballantine, 1980. Print.*

Here are eight life lessons from the early life of Theodore Roosevelt:

1. Never underestimate the power of early education.

Because he was an ill child, Roosevelt was confined to bed and home. He learned at an early age to fill his mind with reading. Coming from a family of means, his father took him and his family to visit sights and museums from Western Europe to the Middle East. He became acutely aware of the world beyond his home in New York and easily became fluent in other languages.

Lesson: You never know what future leader you may be developing when you expose a young mind to opportunities to learn deeply.

2. Never underestimate the influence of strong parental values.

Theodore developed some strong tendencies to vigorous habits. His father was incredibly self-disciplined and young Teddy developed similar habits of hard-work, tenacity, and moral conviction. These traits followed him through life and gave him an ability to fiercely confront acts of dishonesty or corruption.

Lesson: The legacy of a great leader often begins when an adult mentor models those qualities first.

3. Never underestimate the benefits of vigorous self-improvement.

When Teddy was a young teen, his family doctor told him he had a sharp mind but a weak body. He encouraged him to develop the mind since he couldn't do both.

His father refused to accept this and turned one floor of their home into a gym. The result was a young Theodore who worked out so vigorously in muscle building, running, and boxing, that he became a specimen of physical health while still maintaining a love for reading and earning.

Lesson: Robust physical health not only makes you feel better, it provides amazing energy for learning.

4. Never underestimate the value of Providence.

The stories of coincidence, fortune, or luck for Roosevelt are hard to explain as anything but providential. Yes, he was a hard worker, a great student, an ardent politician, and an adventuresome explorer/outdoorsman.

But his survival of battles—whether physical, political, or military—were amazing. For example, as a boy he overcame chronic illness to become one of strongest and most robust men to serve as President. I would encourage you to read the accounts yourself since they are so unbelievable.

Lesson: It is a healthy practice to recognize how often our lives are touched by circumstances that verge on the impossible if not seen as providential.

5. Death is not always the end; sometimes it is the beginning.

Roosevelt understood the depths of grief. He lost his father at an early age. And he suffered the loss of his first wife and mother on the same day.

These losses, however, seemed to cause him a

motivation to throw himself into new work and pursuits.

Grief is what drove him to go west—a decision that forever changed his understanding of the American west as well as changed his understanding of others and himself.

Through his suffering, he learned lessons that would shape him as a man and future President.

Lesson: Sometimes our most creative, productive achievements are born out of our deepest times of loss.

6. Publicity is a powerful promotional tool.

Starting his adult life in state politics, Roosevelt soon learned the power of the press. Whenever he met obstacles or needed public awareness, he used his relationship with the press to further those causes.

Sometimes this backfired, and he became the focus point of critical editorials. But more often than not, he learned how to promote issues of importance to influence policy changes or affect public opinion.

Lesson: Communication of your ideas with a vast

audience is a great way to grow momentum for a worthy cause.

7. A solitary focus on your enemies, instead of friends, will lead to an inevitable dead end.

Not all of Roosevelt's tendencies were admirable. As police commissioner of New York City, he learned the painful lesson of unilateral decision-making.

During this assignment, he reacted with furious tirades at a fellow commissioner's resistance to his reforms. His tendency to bully his way backfired, and the resulting stalemate kept him from seeing any further improvements there.

This painful lesson served him well in future posts. Although still fiercely independent, he learned the value of seeking consensus from others in order to push ahead positive reforms.

Lesson: Learning to count your cost before a battle, even by seeking common ground with those who may resist you, is a smarter path to change than one-man victories.

8. Courage is inspiring.

Finally, Roosevelt's personal courage truly made him remarkable. Whether it was taking on bosses in his own Republican Party, going fist-to-cuff with bullying statesmen, chasing down and arresting thieves in the Wild West, or leading Calvary-men on deadly but victorious charges, he never hesitated to fight a good fight.

Behind each of these instances was a motivation that was often greater than personal promotion. If you believe his own words and journals, Roosevelt truly believed it was worth fighting evil or corruption to promote the common good.

And he didn't mind the thrill of it either.

Lesson: When you are confronted by difficulty, remember that your response affects not only the situation but how those around you may respond to their own difficulties. Make it a courageous response.

Wrap It Up

Theodore Roosevelt's early life is both inspiring and challenging. He is a man who accomplished more in his early years than most of us will in our lifetime.

But his example shows us truths from which we can all benefit. He learned deep lessons from his wrestling with grief, understood the power of communication, benefited from defeats as well as victories, and often chose the more difficult paths when he knew they were the right ones.

As a result, he made a difference. With God's help, we can make a difference too.

Now It's Your Turn

How have you learned to turn difficulties into opportunities? Share with someone one way you have grown through adversity.

Chapter 15

Your Vacation Is Still Important

———— ~ ————

For educators, the need for vacation is a no-brainer. But as a school leader, you will find it more and more difficult to carve out time to get away.

Believe me, when you have positions to fill, reports that are due, and fires to put out, taking off can often be more stressful than just working.

Nevertheless, you need time off to rejuvenate. Rest is something we often forget can make us more productive.

Regardless of whether someone is an educator or not, or whether your vacation time is long or short, taking time away from work is healthy for a number of reasons:

1. Vacation reminds you of who you really are.

Sometimes it is too easy to identify one another by our work. When we introduce ourselves to someone new, we almost always end up explaining what work we do. That's not bad, but it also exemplifies how common it is to build our identities around our work.

Getting away for personal or family time allows us to come back to some of the priorities motivate us to do good work.

It gives me time to see my children play, to explore together, to read books, to have longer conversations with my wife, and to pray.

All of these connections help me rediscover what is important and ultimately give more meaning to my work when I return.

2. Vacation allows you mental and emotion de-tox.

There is something healthy about days of not accomplishing work-related projects, reading emails, answering questions, solving problems, attending meetings, etc.

Like exercising different muscles in your body helps you discover where you need to gain strength, vacation allows you to exercise different mental and emotional muscles. It gives your brain and psyche a break from its normal "work-out".

3. Vacation stimulates creativity.

On vacation I find time for those areas I love that may often get ignored. I find myself having more time to write, play music, travel, or spend time with friends and family.

For instance, one morning during a Colorado vacation, I was able to reflect on my surroundings and write the following:

This morning the panorama of mountains is breathtaking. Peaks in the distance show ridges still covered with snow. The jagged, gothic, jutting, massive gray of a 14-er hides behind the closer green aspen covered hills.

Mountains to my north and east alternate with colors of green and exposed red dirt and bare rock. And meadows below them all are covered with wildflowers: brilliant yellows, whites, and purples.

As I write this, humming birds are alternating between

feeders nearby--shimmering greens, browns, and ruby-throated buzzing back and forth.

Yesterday morning, I saw a deer bouncing away in the meadows below. And two nights ago, we watch as a copper colored fox prowled around looking food treasures.

These kind of reflective moments are possible outside of vacation too, but getting away is also a great time to experience them.

4. Vacation creates great memories.

One of my teammates at school has a great practice of putting his vacation photos on his laptop computer as a screen saver. He keeps it nearby his desk during the day. When he has time to work at his desk, vacation memories consistently greet him.

Although we should never live simply for the pleasure

of playing, vacation is a great way to rediscover your priorities, detox mentally, stimulate creativity, and create new memories.

Wrap It Up

As you carry the weight that comes with school leadership, don't forget to take time to get away and reflect on what is important, de-clutter your mind, stimulate creativity, and return with some favorite memories. Rest reminds you of the importance of making life count --in and out of school.

Now It's Your Turn

What are some of your favorite vacation memories this year? How can you use those memories as ways for students or teammates to learn more about what motivates you?

---~---

Part 4

Building For Growth

---~---

Chapter 16

'First Days Of School' Questions

———————— ~ ————————

Each summer you will spend time revising handbooks, hiring or replacing staff/teachers, determining next year's budget, and managing the master schedule as you prepare for students to return.

One of my favorite books to recommend to new teachers is Harry Wong's *First Days of School*.[10]

In it, he outlines the essentials for establishing, organizing, and implementing good routines and procedures for students.

I call his approach "teaching with both sides of your

---

[10] *Wong, Harry K. - Rosemary T.Wong - Chelonnda Seroyer – The First Days Of School: How To Be An Effective Teacher. Harry K. Wong Publications, 2009.*

brain" or "teaching with one hand while managing with the other."

Wong likes to remind teachers of seven things students will want to know on the first day of school:

> *"Am I in the right room? Where am I supposed to sit? Who is the teacher as a person? Will the teacher treat me as a human being? What are the rules in this classroom? What will I be doing this year? How will I be graded?"*

Learning to manage and instruct at the same time is key to a great classroom. These dual priorities are also the key to leading a strong school or organization.

When I took my first position as an assistant principal, my superintendent at the time had also been a longtime veteran elementary teacher.

When I asked her for advice on school leadership, her response was practical but very wise. She said, "Think of every setting–whether you are with children or adults–as a classroom."

In other words, adults are no different than students when it comes to the need to know what to expect.

With that in mind, here are seven questions we should anticipate our teachers or staff will have before the first days of school:

1. *What is my schedule?*
2. *What extra duties or assignments might I expect?*
3. *Who is my supervisor or administrator as a person?*
4. *Will he/she treat me as a human being?*
5. *What are the expectations, procedures, policies in our school?*
6. *What am I expected to accomplish this year?*
7. *How will I be evaluated?*

Whether it is in the classroom or school-wide, all of us thrive on routine.

That is why we learn schedules, establish arriving/departing routines, create calendars in advance, provide observation/evaluation instruments in advance, and maintain and consistently support policies and procedures.

Otherwise, the alternative is chaos. And chaos is not fertile ground for learning or teaching.

How do answer these questions for our teams? Instead of giving you details on every task you will accomplish before school, let me explain this like we would for students: Keep it simple. Use both sides of your brain. Instruct and manage.

Run your school or organization like a good classroom. Ask yourself what are the qualities, routines, and preparation of your favorite and most effective teachers? Then remember those same skills, routines, expectations, and preparation make strong school-wide climates too.

Just as we take children from different backgrounds and skill levels, and teach and guide them toward common goals and outcomes—the same can be true of every setting.

Wrap It Up

Whether it is a board meeting, public speaking, faculty meetings, parent conferences, or first days of school, don't forget the simple but wise advice that good leadership is simply good teaching.

Now It's Your Turn

What are some ways you have learned to establish and communicate expectations within your organization, school or team?

Chapter 17

Key Responsibility Areas

———————～———————

As you manage a school, you will realize it is always a work in progress.

One of the common traits I have noticed in schools where I have been is the tendency for people to be overwhelmed with so many tasks that they end up distracted from their main job responsibilities.

Whether for you are leading a school team, or you are a team member who wants to more effective, it is important for everyone to know his or her role.

Important Versus Urgent

In Dave Ramsey's *Entreleadership*,[11] he describes the

———————————————

[11] *Ramsey, Dave. Entreleadership: 20 Years of Practical Business Wisdom from the Trenches. New York: Howard Books, 2011. Print.*

difference between "urgent" and "important" tasks. The urgent is often where we focus most of our energy because people want quick solutions. The important is where we must stay focused because we need to accomplish our main mission.

Sometimes the urgent and important are the same, but often they are not. The urgent is not always the most important, and if we forget this, then we end up neglecting our key responsibilities.

Understanding Key Responsibility Areas

Ramsey manages a team of 300+ professionals in his business, and to ensure they accomplish their goals, he provides each of them with KRA's or Key Results Areas. I like to call them Key Responsibility Areas. KRA's become the team members' guide so they stay focused on keeping the "main thing the main thing."

For instance, at the school level, an important role I must play is supervising, observing, and evaluating teachers. Effective instruction, classroom management, and curriculum development are key for ensuring that students are learning. Because of this, I have to make classroom visits a priority.

To accomplish spending adequate time in each classroom, I schedule my visits for the entire year in advance. When someone needs to see me with another urgent matter, they are not ignored. But if I already have my key tasks scheduled in advance, they may have to wait.

Another example of identifying key responsibilities has been with my office staff. At the start of the year, we sat down together and listed every area of responsibility each one manages throughout the year.

Identifying KRA's helped us see each person's main tasks and if any adjustments needed to be made in assignments. I put these KRA's in writing, and followed up with a copy to each member. Each person knows their Key Responsibility Area, and we can review these later in the year when we complete staff evaluations.

For instance, below is snapshot of the KRA's for four office positions from my school. Each school is different, so many of their tasks may mean nothing to you or your situation.

But these are examples of areas to which each staff

person agrees in advance is their area of responsibility:

Position #1 Principal Sect.	Position #2 Counseling Sect.
Building Helpdesk items	Backpack food coordinator
Calling Tree	Drop out/transfer codes
Contact for Alarms	Eligibility
Excel Budget Sheet	EOI grades and test scores
Google Calendar	Lockers
Maintain Purchase Orders	Manage counselor schedules
School App Updates	Manage lists per requests
School calendar	New student enrollment
School directory	Progress reports
SecureTech Code	Report cards
Substitutes	Request records
Teacher certification	Schedule conference rooms
Time sheets	SMART reports
	State reporting
	Student record management
	Transcripts
	WAVE

Position #3 Front Desk

Coke machine problems

Drivers Ed registration

Guests/hospitality

Helping manage attendance

Internet Permission form

Junior Chamber coordinator

Mail room put-away

Manage SMART materials

Meals for PT's and PD's

Parking passes

Rotary meeting coordinator

Schedule computer lab

SEAC payroll deductions

Supply orders

Teacher files

Test monitoring

Warm body counts

Wengage Passwords

Position # 4 Attendance Secretary

10-day warning letters

5-day warning letters

Athletic passes, receipts for testing

Attendance records

Daily attendance

Discipline records

Other attendance state reports

Quarterly state reports

Requests for suspension students

Truancy hearing notifications

Of course no amount of prioritizing will ever be

effective without the right people to carry out tasks. Plus, it is always best if the tasks match strength areas of your team.

I am very blessed with staff members who possess the right strengths for the responsibilities they manage.

When readjusting assignments becomes necessary, however, identifying KRA's helps us keep those conversations focused and productive.

Wrap It Up

What are some areas in your school or area of leadership where you know better definitions of responsibility need to be discussed?

On the front end, developing KRA's for yourself and your team can be time consuming. But over the long-term, developing them helps you operate with more effectiveness and peace-of-mind. Ultimately, it allows you to stay focused on the important, not just the urgent.

Now It's Your Turn

What are some practices you use to stay focused on your ultimate priorities? What are ways you have found to keep yourself or your team focused on the most important outcomes, not just the urgent ones?

Chapter 18

Planting, Growing, and Flourishing

———————～———————

As you watch your school growing, you may easily forget the motivation for being in school leadership. So, let me pause here to bring us back full circle.

I have heard motivational speaker/author Jon Gordon speak on more than one occasion (check out his great resources at http://jongordon.com/).

I remember when he was asked: *What should you do if you find yourself unmotivated to face a day's work?*

He responded by saying: *You should plant yourself right where you are and focus on serving those around you instead of on yourself.*

A Story From School

I was reminded of Jon's words one day when a senior student came by to see me.

"Neither of the counselors was free, so I thought you'd be the next best thing," she said as she came into my office.

I laughed and asked her how I could help her.

She was a student I had known since she was a freshman. When we had discovered how much she had struggled through middle school, we had placed her on a mentor team.

That first year we also took her on a trip to our technology school partner, Tulsa Technology, to tour their campuses. She fell in love with idea of going to Tech, and as a senior, she is enrolled in their dental tech program.

Now she looked worried.

"I am struggling in math and wonder if I can have a

schedule change," she said.

"Oh, what math are you in this year?" I asked.

"Trig," she said, "And I am having a hard time understanding."

Now I was worried. Trigonometry is a tough class, and I didn't know if she had the skill set for such an advanced class. But I tried not to look worried.

"Well, Trig is hard. But I believe if you can see your teacher for some tutoring, that may help," I explained.

"Oh, I am already seeing her for tutoring in the mornings, but I am still struggling."

Now I was even more worried.

"Well," I explained, "We are already weeks in the semester, so we have stopped making schedule changes. How low is your grade in that class?"

"I'm making a B, but I want to make all A's."

Now I was stunned.

"You're making a B in Trig?!" I said with eyes wide open. "That's amazing! Trig is a rigorous class with high expectations. If you're making a B, you are...a rock star!!"

Suddenly, her expression completely changed to one of relief.

"Really?" she said with a smile. "But I wanted to make all A's this year, though, and now I don't think I will. Do you think that's okay?"

So I started reminding her of the big picture: The obstacles she had overcome to get here...how great her grades had been once she had committed to a plan...how more impressed colleges would be with a B in Trig rather than an A in an easier math choice.

Suddenly, she was getting excited about Trig. We had a great conversation and ended our talk with a high-five.

I treasured the talk because it was evidence she had grown into exactly the kind of student I had wanted to see her become. She was no longer the "at-risk" student; she had become the high-achieving student.

Wrap It Up

If you find yourself running low on motivation, look around. Someone needs you to plant a seed of encouragement, vision, or direction for him or her.

Our planting started with the above student years before. Her teachers sowed the seeds of hope that she could have a brighter future. Her mentor team, including a teacher an older student, met with her weekly to check on her grades, to congratulate and challenge her. Her counselor coached her to set high expectations on her schedule each semester.

We planted. She grew. She's flourishing.

And now we are reaping the benefits.

Jon Gordon is right. Help others flourish. And in the process, you may find yourself flourishing too.

Now It's Your Turn

What are ways you have found more joy and motivation in what you are doing? What are some books or resources you would share if someone wanted inspiration to stay motivated? Check our Jon Gordon's book, The Seed, if you want inspiration.

Chapter 19

Communicating About Your School

———— ~ ————

Recently, I saw a great Twitter feed quote: *Communication is 100% of what a principal does.*

Although this may seem like an exaggeration, I believe it is true of almost all educators--especially school leaders who want to build excellent schools.

Earlier this school year when I was attending a school event, a parent stopped me to say thanks for a recent group email I had sent. Then another parent stopped me and said the same. Then I received a nice thank-you email the next day too.

Believe me, I still receive lots emails, phone calls, and visits about concerns, but it is refreshing to also receive positive feedback from parents. And I am convinced this doesn't happen by accident.

When it comes to communication, there is no silver bullet, but there are many tools you can use. Based on the practices at my school, here is a list of 10 ways you can keep those lines of positive communication open with your parents, students, and community:

1. Group Email to Parents

This is by far one of the most popular means of communication I have used. One of my tech-savvy assistant principals showed me how to filter through our data information system for all parent emails. I also have a collection of addresses I gathered from ones teachers have shared with me.

Once a week I try to send out a newsy email about school happenings. If you do this, place the parent email addresses in the Bcc tab to protect privacy.

2. Daily announcements

There are lots of ways to do daily announcements. We try to keep our over-the-speaker ones to a minimum amount of time. Instead we post a full list as a PowerPoint that runs in our commons all day on a big-screen monitor. My secretary also emails the daily bulletin to teachers, parents and students who request to receive it.

3. Newsletters

If you can, dedicate one person to receive all emails about student/teacher successes. We have a teacher with an elective hour dedicated to producing a newsletter that is posted online, and we print copies to keep in offices for guests to see.

4. Website headlines

Keep news updated on your website. Our district technology director will post special announcements and/or student highlights on the website homepage. Teachers with their own websites can have their web addresses linked to our school page too.

5. Teacher emails

This is one of the easiest ways to communicate information to everyone at once. Not only do I email my teachers regularly, but many of them send out weekly communications to parents. Some of them use Remind101, Twitter, or Edmodo as quick ways to text reminders to students too.

6. Being visible

Want people to know you support them? Be in hallways, classrooms, and at special events, games, and community gatherings. It means a lot to students, parents, teachers, and patrons.

7. Students of the month

Have your teachers nominate and vote on a boy and girl from each grade. Our students receive certificates and get their photos shared via our multiple media options. The students love the recognition and their parents do too.

8. Celebrations

Be creative in making a big deal about success. We host an annual breakfast for all students who are successful in state exams, celebrate teacher birthdays once a month with cake in the teacher lounge, recognize student achievement at spirit assemblies, and make announcements when great things happen–to name a few ways to celebrate.

9. Networking

Whether it is blogging, professional associations, or agreeing to speak or present at an area conference, you don't just represent yourself. You are also an ambassador for your school or organization. Don't be afraid to talk to fellow school leaders and others about what's happening at your school. Networking is encouraging and motivating.

10. Posting calendars online

Keep your school calendar on the school website as well as the district calendar. It is a helpful resource for anyone wanting to know what's happening at the school.

Wrap It Up

Whether it is parent relations, teacher observations/evaluations, student relations, staff leadership, community involvement, networking or even doing state reports—all require engaging others, showing appreciation, working as a team, celebrating successes, or giving helpful feedback.

And people appreciate it when you give them feedback. When you are intentional about keeping people informed, they will value and appreciate the great things happening in your school. And it will keep you excited and focused on the positives, not just the challenges of school leadership.

Now It's Your Turn

What are some of your favorite tools for communicating with your teachers, students, fellow teammates, parents, patrons or clients? What is one new way you will start communicating now?

Chapter 20

Lessons From A Crosswalk Guard

———— ～ ————

This past year, my two youngest children started walking to and from school.

On the first day, they were excited to tell us about their favorite crossing guard: Mr. Charlie, a grandfatherly man who stops each child to introduce himself.

He talked so long that first day, they began to fear they would be late to school. He was equally glad to see them on their way home.

Mr. Charlie is the first and last impression of school they encounter each day.

Not long ago, they told me they were on their walk home from school when they came to the last crosswalk. Suddenly, they realized Mr. Charlie wasn't there. They stopped and looked at one another. One by one the children behind them began to pile up. None of them had ever crossed without Mr. Charlie before.

Finally, one of them blurted out, "What are we going to do!?"

"I don't know," said another.

"We're going to die!" one began to wail.

"No, we're not. We just have to cross."

Finally, a small girl asked. "Who's the oldest? Hold up your hands!"

The rest obeyed.

"Ok," she said. "You cross first and we'll follow you."

"Ok," said an older kid. "Ready, let's cross."

And so after looking both ways, in unison and all screaming together 'We're going to die', they crossed over safely to other side.

It made for a great story that evening. And of course, we were relieved to hear the next day that Mr. Charlie was back at his post

They didn't have the nerve to ask what had happened to him the day before.

When I heard the story of Mr. Charlie, I was reminded what an important part he plays in the lives of the children in his charge.

Sometimes he makes them laugh with comments like, "If you paid your mom, she might give you a ride tomorrow." But mostly, he marks the start and end of their daily school routine. He makes them feel safe. He helps them believe all is all right in the world.

As we go about the business of doing school, we can never underestimate the power of the role each of us plays in the lives of others.

A Story From My Past Teaching Days

Years ago, I ran into a graduate from one of the schools where I had taught. He came up to me and said, "Mr. Parker. Do you remember me?"

"Yes, I said. Remind me your name," which is what I almost always say when trying to remember the name of the thousand or more students whom I have taught.

"I'm Anthony," he said, shaking my hand. "I wanted to tell you thanks. You probably don't remember, but each day of class my freshman year, you would say, 'I'm glad to see you today.' It was a small thing but meant a lot to me. In fact, one night I had been in a fight with my parents. I ended up sleeping outside, covered by newspaper to stay warm, and when I dragged into your first hour that morning, you met me with a smile and said you were glad I was there. It was exactly what I needed to hear, and it helped me a lot. So thanks."

It was one of those moments where I was speechless. I thanked him for saying hello, shook hands with him again, and found out how life was going for him.

I didn't know it then, but I had been his Mr. Charlie that year, and it made him feel safe, took away his fear of the unknown, and made him feel everything was going to be okay.

Wrap It Up

Who are you being a Mr. Charlie for each day this year? My guess is there is more than one student or co-worker you walk by every day who could benefit from your greeting or smile. There are people whose lives are better when you are on time, prepared, and happy to see them.

Whether we are elementary age, high school age, or adults, we can all benefit from being a little more like Mr. Charlie.

Now It's Your Turn:

What are some of the routines you can practice each day to helps set the tone for your students or team?

Chapter 21

Lessons from a 10-year-old

———⁓———

Tobias, a 10 year-old Oklahoma boy, wrote a letter to a local TV station because he had a dream for his 11-year-old brother who has Cerebral Palsy.

He asked if they could spread the word that he wanted to borrow a large jogging stroller for a local 5k run that was coming up.

Tobias's dream was to push his brother through the race, but their single mom could not afford to buy a jogging stroller.

Of course, when the news station spread the word, a sponsor quickly donated the stroller, and Tobias's run and story were broadcast on the evening news (see http://www.news9.com/story/23543509/young-boy-reaches-out-to-news-9-for-help).

When asked by a local reporter why this was so important to him, Tobias said, "When I run, I can be his legs." Then he added, "I can be the legs, not just for him but for others too."

Sometimes the simplest gestures can be incredibly moving. One of the greatest ways leaders can help is by supporting others.

With Tobias's example in mind, here are five simple reminders of how you can provide support to your school:

1. Moral Support

A college mentor once told me, "Time spent equals relationship built." So being present, attending events, stopping for conversations, letting people know when you are proud of them—all of these steps let people on your team know you are interested in, care about, and support their work.

When times get tough, it is a lot easier to reach for goals in an environment of support.

2. Listening

Whether you have student in need, a teacher dealing with a difficult situation, or a parent with a concern, author Stephen Covey's maxim can be very helpful: "We must first seek to understand before seeking to be understood."

Taking time to listen, helping find solutions, and affirming that a person's concerns are important—each of these gestures can help reduce anxiety and often make a tough situation just a little easier to handle.

Much more could be said about the power of listening, but keep it simple. Stop what you are doing, give your undivided attention, and really try to understand the people who are bringing you their concerns.

3. Coaching/Training

There is some great training available for those interested in growing professionally. Whether it is a conference, a webinar, inviting a trainer, or hiring substitutes so that new teachers can spend time observing and learning from veteran teachers—all of us benefit from the opportunity to keep learning.

It is so beneficial to learn for teachers to learn from master teachers and to collaborate with teachers within their own subject areas. With the advent of webinars, opportunities to learn are more plentiful than ever.

As school leaders, we need to encourage and make these opportunities available to our teams. Not all of them cost money either. In our state, for instance, teachers who attend summer AP conferences are reimbursed by the state for the time they train. Take time to share from your own expertise too.

4. Resources

Whether it is science lab orders, new technologies, updated literature, or even furniture—your team members have items that will make it easier to accomplish your shared goals.

A site budget priority should first be to help teachers purchase needed resources each year. In the spring, we gather requests for purchase requests from all of our departments. Then we keep a percentage of our budget free for unforeseen needs.

When visiting with teachers throughout the year, ask them if there is anything they need that can support what they are doing. Whether it is a replacement bulb for a projector or an additional bulletin board, sometimes a simple purchase can go a long way to helping a teacher or staff member.

5. Donations/Grants

When you cannot meet all your needs through a site budget, don't be afraid to ask for outside help. Our district has a wonderful group of community leaders who started a non-profit foundation just for the purpose of awarding grants to local teachers who have creative ideas that may not fit into a normal school budget.

Be creative. You would be amazed how many local

businesses or individuals are interested in helping teachers with needed supplies. For instance, last year we had a local church donate free copy paper to our English department. Every thoughtful donation like this goes a long way in the classroom.

You can also help teachers by making them aware of opportunities for grants. For example, if a teacher is interested in beginning a new AP offering, the College Board provides grant opportunities. Our curriculum director has been a champion in helping teachers to write proposals for needed funding to get new programs started.

Wrap It Up

As school leaders, providing support is one of our main responsibilities. Tobias and his brother teach a lesson we should all embrace as our own. We may not be able to literally run for others, but we can find ways to provide moral support, a listening ear, needed training or access to resources.

Now It's Your Turn

What are some actions you can take today to support others? Choose one and make someone's day that much better.

Chapter 22

Lessons from my Son's Hospital Stay

———————～———————

When my son was eight years old, he was diagnosed and recovered from an infectious disease known as Kawasaki.

He made a complete recovery with no apparent after-effects and is a happy, energetic, and healthy.

In addition to the amazing support of our friends, church and community, I was astounded at the phenomenal care he received from his nurses, techs, doctors, and interns.

Here are four lessons in teamwork I reflected on from our experience with my son's medical team that could apply to schools:

1. A common goal unites a group of diverse people.

To give you some context, when our son was first admitted, he was in terrible shape: high fever, rash, swelling, etc.

When they diagnosed him with Kawasaki and began treatments, his condition worsened.

Then he went into shock.

His treatments had to stop while they stabilized him for the next twenty-four hours. Then they began treatments again, and this time the symptoms began to disappear and he began to heal.

It was obvious during the entire time that his medical team had one goal in mind: to save our son.

No matter their backgrounds, gender, differences in job titles or compensation, each team member was focused on that one outcome. Every decision was weighed against its effect on him, his condition, and well being.

In Jim Collin's book, *Good to Great*, he studies the most

effective businesses in America—ones with the longest track record of success.

And one of many contributing factors was the ability of great companies to focus on a specific area where they can be most effective and work toward that goal.

Lesson learned? When we focus on a common goal, not allowing ourselves to be distracted by secondary ones, we are more strategic and effective. What is the common goal you are working toward with your team? A common goal can unify the most diverse of people into positive action.

2. Great team members know their roles and execute them well.

Whether it was the nurse tech assigned to check my son's vitals, his RN who was determined to bring his fever under control, his physicians prescribing treatments or the pharmacists or lab techs we never met but who were prescribing or analyzing—each one played a pivotal role in his healing.

And each one performed the role assigned. The nurse did not attempt diagnose. That was the doctor's role. The tech did not administer meds. That was the nurse's role. Instead, each person performed the role he or she had been assigned.

At an athletic event, you sometimes see a team playing "in the zone". Everything seems to flow effortlessly. But in reality you are observing the skills of individuals who understand their roles and have played them long enough, practiced enough, and been together enough to make a complicated event look like play.

The result is something beautiful to observe.

Lesson learned? Fulfilling specific roles means each team member understands his or her key responsibility areas. When each of us performs our specific role on a team, the effect and outcome can often be breath taking.

3. Caring for people and reaching outcomes must go hand in hand.

Not only did his medical team accomplish the goal of curing our son, but also they truly cared for him.

Whether it was regulating his meds, whispering soothing words, or finding creative ways to relieve fever, they were consistently showing the sincerest care for him.

Most educators are familiar with the research done by the Gates Foundation on the three R's that are present in all great schools: rigor, relevance, and relationship.

In school, an educator may be an expert in curriculum and instruction. But the intangible element of caring for and loving students always separates a good "instructor" from a great "teacher".

Lesson learned? When trust and care are present, not only is a goal accomplished but also a meaningful relationship is established at the same time. And usually more learning, productivity and positive outcomes occur in the process.

4. Great teams remain teach-able.

Another of the reason I think my son's medical team was so effective was that he was in a teaching hospital. Resident doctors interning there were being asked to participate and lead in decision-making. At the same time, the older doctors were mentoring, coaching, and teaching them.

It was an atmosphere of mutual respect where continuous learning, research, and practice were valued.

Not only do you flourish when you work in a culture of learning but also those whom you are serving will flourish too.

Lesson learned? When people value the importance of constantly learning from one another, relying on research-based methodology, and growing through experienced practice, then you have created a culture of learning and growth.

Great things happen in places where people are flexible, open, and teachable.

Wrap It Up

Great teams work for common goals, execute individual roles, care for others, and remain teach-able. In my son's case, the actions of a great team quite literally saved his life. Think about what we can accomplish in our lives, schools or organizations when we do the same.

Now It's Your Turn

What are some other examples of great teamwork you have observed? What would you add to the list of qualities it takes to build a great team?

Part 5
A Place of Belonging

Chapter 23

Managing Grief

———~———

As I was writing this book, our school lost a senior student in a car accident.

She was one of our dream students: cheerleader, great student, fun-loving, and loved by all.

You can imagine the grief and remorse that gripped our school and community during this time. As painful as the time was for our school, I also watched people pull together in some beautiful ways.

A good friend asked me how a school could prepare for something like this. I don't think anyone can ever prepare for the loss of a student, but here is some feedback I shared with him, as he wanted some ideas to share with his school leadership:

1. Communicate, communicate, communicate.

Information is vital for people to cope with grief. As soon as we were able to establish a line of communication in this situation, we did. We had a staff person who was loved and trusted by the family on site as soon as possible.

Frequent messages were relayed back to us. One staff person at the school emailed out those updates so teachers/students could be kept up-to-date. Nothing is more difficult for people in grief than not knowing what is happening, so communicate frequently and factually.

I also took time to send an email to all of our parents attempting to sensitively inform them. I assured them that we would have a team of counselors on hand, and encouraged them that we would patiently and compassionately carry on with as normal a school schedule as possible.

We also held an emergency faculty meeting so everyone was on the same page with understanding what happened and how we would respond.

2. Be present and visible.

As the principal, I felt it important to visit the family as well. So as soon as I could, I was present and available to the family. I kept my time brief, but I wanted to communicate on behalf of the school the sadness and love felt by all for the student and her loved ones.

I also attended a prayer vigil and the funeral and kept in constant communication with a family friend as well as my school and district leaders on what was happening.

We ended up hosting the funeral at the school, which also required some hands on preparations.

Needless to say, many of my other duties were postponed for this priority, but I tried to be as visible as possible throughout the school so teachers and students could sense we were still "doing school" while also responding to the crisis.

3. Maintain as much stability and routine as possible.

A healthy way to manage grief is staying the course. In the

spirit of trying to maintain routines, we cancelled some professional development time we had scheduled that would have brought some substitutes in for some teachers.

Instead we encouraged all of our teachers to be in class so that our week could be "as normal as possible."

Even while we prepared for grief, I encouraged our teachers to teach. Not every student or teacher grieves the same. And some knew the student better than others. Keeping the routine as normal as possible helped school stay on track with a back-up plan for those needing more attention.

4. Allow creative and spontaneous responses.

While maintaining a good routine is important, likewise, you can never predict the kind of responses students will demonstrate or ask to initiate, so remain flexible.

For instance, some volunteers organized an evening prayer vigil. Teachers created signs where students could write love messages and prayers.

Students asked for a school-wide effort to wear a favorite color in memory. They requested a spontaneous group photo at the end of one day and over 300 students participated. We sent the photo as a love message to the family.

One teacher told me that the first day back, her students were unable to speak with the empty desk reminding them of their friend. Finally, one of them asked if they could sign the desk. With sharpies in hand, this began a time of guided and compassionate memory sharing.

Other teachers were able to carry on class as usual as individual students asked to visit or share with others in the counseling office.

Be prepared to play it by ear. Maintain as normal a routine as possible while also allowing room for expressions of sympathy.

5. Ask for help from outside the school.

We were intentional about calling in counselors from our

other schools to be with us the first day after our student's death. In addition, ministers from area churches were allowed to be present for students comfortable in sharing with them.

Having additional, supportive adults in the building was also comforting to parents as they were concerned about their own children's ability to cope at school.

As we coordinated with the funeral home on arrangements, we also leaned on staff and volunteers to help with set-up, sound systems, etc. Our school photo vendor donated a large print of her senior portrait for the family. It was a time where lots of people wanted to lend a hand.

6. Enjoy and appreciate your students.

One of the best ways to soothe the hurt of loss is by paying special attention to the wonderful kiddos you still have in your care. Continue to give them kudos and don't forget to congratulate their successes.

For example, our football team had just made it to playoffs when our student tragedy took place. Even in the midst of grieving, we still celebrated their win. The team was treated to a special dinner. We made a big deal in announcements about their accomplishments. Their coach was our teacher of the month.

Losing someone reminds you to let individual students and teachers know how much they are appreciated.

7. Be prepared for media contact.

It wasn't long before the tragedy made it on the news. We were contacted by at least two different sources wanting details. Thanks to my yearbook teacher, I was prepared with a digital photo the family gave me permission to share. We highlighted the positive response of our students, teachers, and community.

It helped that we had already established good contact with these news sources in the past, so I could trust them to report and not exploit the situation. In fact, their reporting was another kind tribute to her memory.

8. Allow yourself time to grieve.

Times like these often bring back painful memories of former student losses or even personal losses. Don't forget to allow yourself time to grieve in the process of comforting others.

Even though I was not personally close to the student we lost, I still found myself appreciating the comfort and prayers of those closest to me. Taking time to privately acknowledge your own struggle will help you compassionately respond to the struggles others are having.

Wrap It Up

No one is ever really prepared for something as painful as a student death. But one way to show compassion during such a time is to be prepared to support your school community when they are grieving.

Whether that includes communicating, being there, bringing in help, keeping up routines, showing appreciation, managing media contacts, or allowing yourself time to grieve—these are just some of the ways you can positively contribute during a painful time for your school.

Now It's Your Turn

I know some of you have been through similar or perhaps more difficult situations. What are some other ways you could be better prepared to help during such times in your school?

Chapter 24

Hats Principals Must Wear

———— ~ ————

As you make your school a place of belonging, you will find you are required to wear many hats.

Recently, I was asked to speak to a group of teachers who are interested in becoming school principals. My task was to summarize some of the principal's roles and responsibilities.

If you are a principal, I am sure you could add more to my list. If you are thinking of becoming a principal, here are seven hats I believe you should expect to wear:

1. Coach

Someone has to make the final call, and as the principal, that will often be you. Like a good coach, you will need to understand the strengths and weaknesses of your team.

You will need to listen to input from others. But ultimately, you will be the one who often makes many of the final calls in your building.

Coaches also set the tone, cast the vision, or help motivate their teams to action. Even if you are not a pep-talk kind of person, it is important that you are clear with direction, consistent with follow-through, and fair-minded in difficulties. Like it or not, others will look to you for direction and follow your lead. So plan to lead in a positive direction.

2. Manager

School leadership is much more than management, but it is still an important part of it.

Some principals are surprised at the amount of work required for supervision, personnel decisions, report generating, budget decisions, and schedule planning. If you are transitioning from the classroom, you are now responsible for an entire school.

You can't manage a school without a great team.

One way I have tried to encourage focus in office management of our school, for instance, is by putting job responsibilities in writing. Each office staff member has key responsibility areas in writing so each of us know who is managing specific tasks throughout the year.

3. Counselor

Whether it is handling concerns of students, parents, teachers, or other school staff, a significant part of school leadership is learning to listen. I am not a counselor and do not pretend to be. But I have learned the importance of giving my attention to someone in need, providing them feedback, and helping them to find solutions.

Sometimes people just need to be heard, and sometimes they need to be guided into finding their own solutions. My favorite Stephen Covey quote always comes into play when I talk about counseling: Seek first to understand before seeking to be understood.

4. On Duty

Like it or not, everyone is accountable to someone. Just because you are a principal does not mean you are on your own. You still answer to your superiors. You still answer to the state department. You still follow the same rules, regulations, policies, and laws your staff is expected to follow.

When you are absent for family sick leave, for instance, you fill out the same form your teachers fill out. I sign in every morning on the same sheet my teachers use for sign in. In fact, I am usually the first one to sign in. Principals are on duty just like everyone else.

5. Chief Communicator

I am not sure I can emphasize enough the importance of keeping people informed. So often because you are on the front end of decisions or information coming to the school, you falsely assume others have the same information or context.

Here are a few ways I try to keep communication clear:

a. Be present and visible.

b. Follow up meetings with email summaries.

c. Email parents and teachers group emails with school updates.

d. When someone is upset, call or see in person if possible.

e. Send photos and updates to your local media outlets.

f. Create a school newsletter so great events are published to a wider audience.

6. Servant-Leader

One aspect I appreciate about my current superintendent is his ability to roll up his sleeves and lend a hand. More than once, he has been seen helping out with grounds work, standing in the serving line at faculty meals, or organizing a tailgate party on game night.

Principals are not exempt from service. In fact, they

should be on the front-line when it comes to helping others. This doesn't mean you neglect the tasks of management, supervision, and meetings to do all maintenance tasks in your building. Instead, it means that at times, you will need to step in when there is a need and lend a hand.

More than once, I have cleaned up the spill in the commons. Working a mop is something I can still do while wearing a tie.

7. Team Player

Finally, a principal must remember he is not working alone. Teachers, students, or staff members who are talented, intelligent and creative surround you. And you always accomplish more when pulling with a team than by yourself.

So you must not forget that you need others to be successful. And other need you too. Strong leaders do not push others. Instead, they lead and are followed.

As you set the tone for your building, remember you are doing this in partnership with others. Reminding yourself that you are part of team will keep you from the false belief that you are on your own. I heard someone say once concerning leaders: Tuck in your cape, you are not a super hero; you are on a team.

Wrap It Up

School leadership is a multifaceted calling whether you are a coaching, managing, staying accountable, communicating, serving, or working with a team. Ultimately, your goal is to create a safe and effective learning environment, no matter what hats you have to wear to reach that goal.

Now It's Your Turn

My list is based on my own experience but it is not exhaustive. What are some other roles or responsibilities school leaders must be prepared to handle?

Chapter 25

Interviewing For An Education Position

───────⌒───────

If you've made it this far in the book, you have come farther than most people do when they pick up a new read. You may have read this book because you are a school leader wanting to grow. Or perhaps you are new to school leadership and wanting feedback from a veteran.

Either way, thank you for taking time to let me share with you.

As you find yourself growing in your profession, you may also find yourself looking for a position that better fits your strengths and callings. So I wanted to take this final chapter to share some tips I have learned from interviewing.

My first year transitioning from assistant principal to site principal, I hired more than a dozen certified positions and an additional eight non-certified ones.

As hard as it is to work through the hiring process, nothing is more important to building a great school than finding quality educators and team players.

Although I haven't kept count, it is safe to say that during the last ten years, I have interviewed over a hundred individuals for staff or teaching positions. I have also sat on teams interviewing for principal or director positions.

As a school administrator, I have seen many great and not-so-great interviews. Likewise, I have delivered some of both.

Perhaps you are looking for that next step in your career. Because I am a teacher at heart, I sometimes visit with candidates afterwards about ways they could improve their interview skills.

Since I find myself coaching the same consistent themes, here are the 10 of them:

1. Write a solid resume.

This should go without saying, but a good resume should be neat, concise, and without errors. Display a heading with all your contact information. Skills most pertinent to the position should be prominent and experience should be listed chronologically with most recent experiences first.

If possible, limit your resume to one-page. Long resumes are tedious to read and usually unnecessary.

2. Pre-emptive email or phone.

My advice is to send a short, friendly email to the person(s) you believe will be responsible for the hiring. This is usually pretty easy to figure out by visiting school websites or just calling and asking school staff for contact information. Make sure your inquiry is brief, professional, and without misspellings.

If you choose to reach someone by phone or leave a voicemail, rehearse what you will say ahead of time. By all means, do not ramble or give the impression that you are desperate for a job. School leaders want people who are passionate about teaching or leading, not about just finding a job.

3. Research your prospects.

With the ease of finding information via the web, there is no excuse for not understanding in advance the lay-of-the-land in respect to the school or community you have targeted. More helpful still is finding someone you may know who lives or works in that community as a source for information.

Coming into an interview knowing a few names and faces helps to put you a step ahead and gives you some context for the discussion you will have.

4. Rehearse your introduction (and deliver with a smile).

Almost all interviews begin with the opportunity for you to introduce yourself personally, professionally, and in regards to your education.

First, express thanks for the opportunity to interview; then, follow-up with a brief introduction of who you are personally and professionally. Sit up straight, smile, and make good eye contact. Avoid crossed arms, clenched fists, or rambling which usually show signs of anxiety.

Appearing cool under pressure is important because that is what you will be expected to do every day in a teaching or school leadership position. I can't tell you how much more attractive candidates appear when they smile, so don't forget your most powerful persuasion tool, which is often your expression.

5. Play to your strengths and come with your A-game.

Your goal in an interview is to demonstrate the same confidence, preparation, and ability to connect that you will need in the classroom or the position you are seeking.

So show up with same A-game in an interview that you would want your students or team-mates to see you deliver everyday in your potential position.

6. Anticipate questions and be prepared with examples.

You will be asked questions about how you define effective teaching or schools, use procedures, handle difficult situations or people, and understand content area.

Expect questions about your willingness or interest in extra-duty assignments, and examples of past experiences. Don't be surprised by these. Think them through in advance. If you are asked a question you never anticipated, take a breath and think about it before responding.

Again, your goal is to demonstrate how you will communicate to students or colleagues on a regular basis, so be clear, concise, and use examples.

7. Turn failures into stepping stones.

A good interview should also be challenging. If you are asked about failures or difficult times in your professional experience, be honest, and share an experience where you turned a difficulty into an opportunity to grow and improve.

8. Bring your own questions.

Write down and bring with you questions of your own.

Here a few examples:

1. *What are the most important qualities you are looking for in this position?*

2. *How would you describe the culture of your staff or school?*

3. *How would you describe your leadership style?*

4. *Can you describe how you lead and support your teachers or team members?*

5. *How soon will you be making a decision about this position?*

Avoid questions about compensation. Those questions

can wait if you're given a follow-up opportunity.

9. Rehearse your closure.

Just as important as your introduction is your final impression.

Take time again to thank your interviewer(s) for the opportunity to meet. Repeat the reasons you believe this position is a great fit for your skills and strengths. Tell them you look forward to hearing from them soon and then stand, offer firm handshakes, and don't forget to smile.

10. Follow-up with an email or card.

If possible within the same day as the interview, send an email or leave a card expressing your thanks for the opportunity to interview.

As hard as it was for you to do the interview, remember your interviewers are giving up hours of time they would normally spend on other priorities to look for the best candidates.

Be patient if they don't quickly respond to you with a follow-up, and do not burn any bridges if you are not offered the position. Every interview is an opportunity to show your strengths and may open another door down the road.

An Additional Resource

A book I have found helpful for both discovering your passions and preparing for good interviews is Dan Miller's *48 Hours To The Work You Love.* He does a great job of giving specific examples of resumes, cover letters, and interview samples.

Wrap It Up

If you take nothing else away from these tips, remember this: Interviews are so much more than a one-time opportunity to speak to someone.

Finding the position you want begins by the quality of performance you are showing at your current position, is reinforced by the kind of responses your co-workers will give when contacted about you, and is enhanced by your ability to deliver when given the opportunity.

No amount of interview preparation will ever be as important as your reputation.

Now It's Your Turn

What are some additional suggestions or tips you find helpful when coaching others on interview to-do's? What are some questions you still may have about interviewing that I haven't addressed?

Epilogue:
Higher Calling

———————～———————

In 2008, American Diane Van Deren won the Yukon Artic Ultra 300. Yes, that's a 300-mile marathon.

Deren's running career began when she discovered the sport helped stave off her epileptic seizures. A brain surgery also left her with the inability to judge time—a quality that has aided her in being able to run amazingly long-distances.

I heard a story about Diane Van Deren that I will paraphrase. Once she was asked to speak to a classroom of disabled children after completing her first 100-mile race, one in which she believed she would never repeat.

After she told her story, a little girl who was wheelchair bound raised her hand.

"Ms. Van Deren," she said. "Could you run your next race for me?"

That comment changed Diane Van Deren forever. She had to run another race. And from then on, she was not only running for her own fulfillment; she was running to inspire and encourage others who struggled with disabilities[12].

Whatever stage you are currently in as a school leader, your ability to finish the race begins with motivation that is bigger than yourself.

In his book *EntreLeadership*[13], Dave Ramsey shares advice for business leaders. His advice applies to school leaders as well:

> Winning…requires that you exhaust every ounce of physical energy you have. You won't put that effort in day in and day out, year in and year out, just for money. Money is great, but it is ultimately an empty goal. Bigger homes, bigger cars, and even more giving is just not a big enough goal to keep you

---

[12] *"Time Out of Mind." YouTube. YouTube: Originally Published via Sports Center, 20 Mar. 2011. Web. <https://www.youtube.com/watch?v=7jATSSgWg-M>.*

[13] *Ramsey, Dave. Entreleadership: 20 Years of Practical Business Wisdom from the Trenches. New York: Howard Books, 2011. Print.*

creative and energized throughout your life. You have to have a passion, a higher calling, to what you engage in.

I have heard many leaders try to motivate educators by telling them that if they don't like their jobs, to change professions. But changing professions will not necessarily help you find fulfillment in your work. Believing in the higher purpose of what you do, however, will keep you grounded when the times get difficult. And believe me, they will be tough.

One final lesson in leadership I want to share comes from the *Bible*.[14] When the followers of Jesus were arguing over who among them would be the greatest, their Teacher sat a child in middle of them as an object lesson of simple humility, and he told them that the one who would be greatest among them must be the one who is willing to be the greatest servant.

Of course, he was describing the pattern of his own life,

---

[14] *"Luke 9: 46-48." ESV Study Bible: English Standard Version. Wheaton, IL: Crossway Bibles, 2010. Print.*

but nevertheless, his lesson on leadership was as counter-cultural then as it is today.

When you lead based on what is best for others, when you strive to provide something valuable for others, when you pull instead of push others along to higher ends, when you sacrifice so other can learn—then you are truly serving others, which in the end is a better investment than any of our retirement accounts.

No matter what the ultimate outcomes are in your school or organization, when you work with the right motivations, then you will also finish well.

Do you have the motivation, courage, action, and teamwork necessary to thrive as a school leader? Even on your best days, you will question whether you do. Remember that it is the sense of calling that will keep you coming back day after day with the right passion, perspective, and purpose.

At the end of the day, being a school leader is not about you. It is about being a part of something so much bigger than you are. It is about serving others with a passionate belief that you are making a difference that will carry on long after you have left your school building.

Being a school leader requires a commitment to serve others—a commitment that is worth it. And one that is possible with the right motivation, a good dose of courage, practical action-steps, and healthy teamwork.

Find Out More About School Leadership at

www.williamdparker.com

If this book has been helpful or you are interested in learning more about school leadership, visit website: Principal Matters at www.williamdparker.com.

I would love to connect with you and provide more feedback or collaborate on ways we can continue to grow as school leaders.

Made in the USA
Lexington, KY
24 February 2016